Sleeping Around

The Bed from Antiquity to Now

"Anything that can't be done in a bed isn't worth doing."
—Groucho Marx

Sleeping Around

The Bed from Antiquity to Now

Annie Carlano & Bobbie Sumberg

Museum of International Folk Art *Santa Fe*

University of Washington Press *Seattle & London*

© **2006 by** the Museum of International Folk Art
Designed by Tom Morin/Context Design Inc.
Typesetting & Production by Theresa Harvey/
Context Design Inc. Galisteo, NM
www.contextdesign.com
Printed by CS Graphics/China

12 11 10 09 08 07 06   5 4 3 2 1

Museum of International Folk Art
PO Box 2087, Santa Fe, NM 87504-2087
www.moifa.org

University of Washington Press
PO Box 50096, Seattle, WA 98145
www.washington.edu/uwpress

Library of Congress Cataloging-in-Publication Data

Carlano, Annie.
Sleeping Around: The Bed From Antiquity To Now/
Annie Carlano and Bobbie Sumberg.
          p. cm.
Includes index.
ISBN 0-295-98598-4 (pbk. : alk. paper)
1. Beds. 2. Bedding. I. Sumberg, Bobbie. II. Title.
NK2713.C37 2006
392.3'6–dc22   2005034676

The paper used in this publication meets the minimum requirements of American National Standard
for Information Sciences—Permanence of Paper
for Printed Library Materials, ANSI Z39.48-1984.

"It was such a lovely day I thought it was a pity to get up."
—*W. Somerset Maugham*

Sleeping Around
Contents

Joyce Ice, *Director*

Museum of International Folk Art

Foreword

Who among us has not relished the scent of fresh linens or the warmth of a cozy bed? The delight of awakening on a summer's morning to the sun streaming across one's bed? The memory of sharing a bedroom with a sibling? The physical act of sleeping is bound up with preverbal memories and sensory experiences from the earliest stages of life. The instinct to protect a sleeping child, to hold a loved one in sleep, is surely hardwired into the human psyche.

This need—both physical and psychic—for the renewal that comes from sleep impels humans to an amazing variety of sleeping arrangements. Because we spend up to a third of our time in bed, it is perhaps not surprising that we also devote large amounts of time and energy—not to mention large sums of money—to achieving a good night's sleep. Witness the development of centers for sleep disorders and the profusion of new pharmaceutical products that promise more peaceful and restful sleep. The immense selection of mattresses on the market today attests to a great interest in comfort, durability, and just the right degree of firmness.

From ages past, people have elaborated upon basic necessity to create comfortable and attractive spaces to aid and enhance rest and slumber. Sleep takes place in an incredible array of settings—shaped by cultural influences, belief systems, demands of climate, and natural surroundings. Bedding, furniture, and other aspects of the setting are embellished by creative impulses, from functional simplicity to ornate decoration.

This fascinating topic has been the subject of research over several years and on several continents as authors and curators Annie Carlano and Bobbie Sumberg have examined material culture and designs related to sleeping, beds, and textiles. They show us a trajectory of ideas reflecting people's ever-changing attitudes and practices concerning sleep and the items considered appropriate and conducive to it. They trace exchanges related to bedding and furniture that cultures widely dispersed across time and space have made through trade and contact.

Along the way they offer tantalizing glimpses of people at their most innocent, intimate, and sensual—in bed. Their expertise and their enthusiasm for the subject matter will appeal to readers as they share insights gleaned from studies in the field as well as from previous research. They skillfully bring these perspectives together in a lively discourse.

Although this publication breaks new ground, it can also be seen as characteristic of the research, programs, exhibitions, and publications produced by the dedicated staff at the Museum of International Folk Art. Cross-cultural and transnational in scope, the work draws upon interdisciplinary perspectives ranging from art history and anthropology to textile studies, decorative arts, and cultural history. It transcends national borders and artificial divisions as it underscores what humans across the world share in common. At the same time, the authors explore variations in artistic and functional responses to the task of creating a safe and comfortable setting for sleep, showing readers the tremendous human capacity for invention and adaptation.

"To sleep, perchance to dream..."
—William Shakespeare

Annie Carlano

Preface

The origin of this book goes back twenty years, to a casual conversation I had with Sarah Buie in New Haven, Connecticut. She proposed an exhibition and book about textiles made for beds, noting that the 1966 landmark show *The Bed* at the Museum of Contemporary Crafts (now the Museum of Arts and Design) in New York was about beds but not about the bedding that made them come alive. With so many of the world's great textiles having been made to adorn bed furniture, and so many of the world's beds constructed of plaited and woven fibers, the need for a book that would bring together the most fascinating of these traditions was evident.

"Bed" continued to be a topic of discussion among my colleagues and me for almost ten years, until finally, at the Museum of Fine Arts, Boston, Cliff Ackley, Ellenor Alcorn, Edward (Ned) S. Cooke, Jr., Peter Lacovara, and Anne Nishimura Morse lent me their expertise to develop an exhibition around the concept. Ultimately, the endeavor we so ambitiously envisioned was too costly—borrowing great beds from China, for example—and eventually we held only a small show in what is now the museum's Loring Textile Gallery. Titled *Sweet Dreams,* it was about textiles from around the world, historic to contemporary, that were made for or as bedding and about costumes designed for wearing to bed. More of a teaser than a blockbuster, that exhibition and its accompanying brochure nonetheless provided the primary impetus and foundation for this book.

Timely ideas gain momentum. Academic conversations about beds and related textiles led staff in the Graduate Studies program at the Fashion Institute of Technology, SUNY, New York City, to add a seminar called "The Bed" to the curriculum in museum studies in 1991. In 1993, a symposium titled "The Bedroom from the Renaissance to Art Deco" was held in Toronto. Its published proceedings, *The Bed from the Renaissance to Art Deco,* edited by Meredith Chilton (Toronto: Decorative Arts Institute, 1993), disseminated the lectures presented there to a wider audience. It became a springboard for more research on the part of furniture and textile historians into the minutiae of inventories and extant objects. On the heels of the Toronto symposium, in 1995, French colleagues published the book *Rêves d'alcôves: La chambre au cours des siècles* and staged the eponymous exhibition at the Musée des Arts Décoratifs, Paris.

Their investigations, though chiefly historical, spilled into the more contemporary sphere. Drawn to the most intimate and yet grandiose of furniture, the bed, Western scholars were not immune to the pervading cultural mores of "cocooning" and other forms of rampant domesticity that began in the United States in the 1980s and reached their apotheosis in the 1990s with the popularity of magazines and television shows about home design, food, cooking, and lifestyle, not to mention the ever-expanding empire of Martha Stewart. From the late 1990s into the current century, cable television and DVDs brought *Sex and the City* not only to Americans but also to a great portion of the rest of the world through dubbing and subtitles. Recognized as a critical obsession of urban and teen life, the topic of sex is no longer taboo—indeed, it is so ubiquitous that it has become blasé. Could this book have been called *Sleeping Around* in the pre–*Sex and the City* world?

The new generation of specialists that emerged in the mid-1980s has been, I think, influenced by such cultural trends personally and professionally. These people have steadily made their mark. In the scholarly world, the London Arts and Humanities Board created a Centre for the Study of the Domestic Interior, a joint program of the Royal College of Art and the Victoria and Albert Museum, which is now spearheading major projects, from fellowships to symposia. Inspired by such actions, and by the public's even stronger desire for home and comfort since the horror of September 11, 2001, the war in Iraq, and other world events, researchers of the "minor," "decorative," and "traditional" arts and material culture are now talking to a wider and more engaged audience. Writing about "the arts that are life" and organizing exhibitions that strike an avuncular cord—with themes such as the quilts of Gees Bend, the Amish, home life during the Great Depression, an intimate look at the young King Tut, and, most recently at the Museum of International Folk Art, beds from Asia to Europe in the exhibition *Dream On*—these scholars have turned the "minor" not just into the major but into the popular. We offer *Sleeping Around* in that spirit.

"In bed my real love has always been the sleep that rescued me by allowing me to dream." —*Luigi Pirandello*

Annie Carlano &
Bobbie Sumberg

Acknowledgments

We could not have written this book alone. Writing may be a solitary activity, but the exacting research that goes into a book like this, and the blood, sweat, and tears that go into its production, are group efforts. Three scholars, Kim Hartswick, Peter Lacovara, and Tamara Tjardes, contributed their fine research, and they have our deepest thanks. Much of the information in this book was gathered at the National Art Library, Victoria and Albert Museum, and we are grateful for the kind assistance of the staff there. Also at the Victoria and Albert Museum, curators Nick Humphrey and Sarah Medlam guided us through the furniture archives.

Françoise Bekus of the Musée National des Arts et des Traditions Populaires, Paris, was extremely generous with her time and assistance, coordinating work in the collections, archives, and library. In Provence, Michel Biehn, Francine Nicolle, and A. J. Cababnel shared their textile expertise. In Florence, Italy, Eve Borsook of Villa I Tatti, Harvard University Center for Italian Renaissance Studies and in Rome, Stefania Masari of the Museo Nazionale delle Arti e Tradizioni Poplari, and Carolyn Valone provided much assistance and many insights. Work in Turkey could not have been carried out without the knowledge and assistance of Vedat Karadağ, Josephine Powell, and Harald Boehmer. At Flou, we thank Anna Casati in Milan, Brigitte Lacroix in Montreal, and Leslie Ventura in New York.

Jeff Spurr and Andras Riedlmayer of the Aga Khan Program, Fine Arts Library, Harvard University, lent their enthusiastic assistance with picture research. Significant research on contemporary beds was carried out across the street at the Loeb Library of the Graduate School of Design, where the entire staff was kind and helpful. Traude Gavin, Bernard Sellato, Hanne Veber, Nicholas Dow, Bernhard Ackermann, and Jeff Cunningham answered questions and supplied vital information.

Acquiring the illustrations and permissions was a major undertaking in itself. Thanks are due to all the institutions and individuals who provided the images without which this book would not have been the same. In particular, Alicia Fessendon of Art Resource helped find many images. Barbara Moore at the Library of Congress, Kay Peterson of the Archives Center National Museum of American History, Kate Igoe at the National Air and Space Museum, and Dave Burgevin with the Smithsonian were very helpful and prompt in their dealings with us. Individuals at the National Czech and Slovak Museum and Library, the Indiana Historical Society, the Long Island Museum of American Art and Carriages, and Monticello all responded in a timely manner to last-minute requests. Original photography of pieces in the collection of the Museum of International Folk Art was ably carried out by Blair Clark, Paul Smutko, Addison Doty, and Margot Geist.

Friends, family, and colleagues whose interest, enthusiasm, and support made this project possible deserve our heartfelt thanks. They include Tom Appelquist, Véronique Balon, Kimberley Davenport, Josiane and Daniel Fruman, Agnes Fruman and Antoine Lorgnier, Francesca Galloway, Mamie Gasfal, Edward M. Gomez, Joss Graham,

Titi Halle, Barry Haywood, Catherine Kurland, Stéphanie Molinard, Dave Morgan, Pip Rau, Valerie Steele, Spencer Throckmorton, Susan Ward, Lauren Whitley, Jeffrey Wolf, Jim and Ben Wright, Jim Zivic, and several Sumbergs.

At the Museum of International Folk Art, we received administrative assistance from Cate Feldman and volunteers Jack Levin, Ava Fullerton, and Pat Harlow. Colleague Felicia Katz Harris used her powers of persuasion to negotiate several sensitive image requests. The ever-cheerful Ree Mobley handled interlibrary loans, preliminary proofreading, and camaraderie. Paul Smutko and Rosemary Sallee of the collections staff were always there when we needed them, which was often. Jacqueline Duke and Laura May handled the complex financial arrangements. We are most grateful to Joyce Ice, director, for her patience and for bringing this project to the attention of the University of Washington Press.

Director Pat Soden and managing editor Marilyn Trueblood of the University of Washington Press proved to be true partners in this joint venture. Jane Kepp, copyeditor, and Tom Morin, graphic designer—a genius and a gentleman—exerted their considerable skills to make this book as readable and as beautiful as you find it.

Books are expensive. We thank the International Folk Art Foundation (IFAF) not only for grants for research in France and Turkey but also for funds to support the publication of this book, as well as for ongoing financial and moral support. We are grateful to the Folk Art Committee of the Museum of New Mexico Foundation for its support of research abroad, to the Margie E. Murdy Foundation and Lloyd Cotsen for contributing to this project, and to Eugenie and Lael Johnson for additional assistance.

Sleeping Around

The Bed from Antiquity to Now

introduction

Annie Carlano

Introduction

Everybody sleeps. Sleep is a biological imperative for humans, as it is for all other mammals. Even as embryonic beings, we sleep in the watery protection of our mother's womb. Human beings started out, not unlike other members of the animal kingdom, gathering or manipulating the natural materials at hand in an attempt to make safe and comfortable places to sleep. The first bed was the earth itself, from dirt or sand to soft grass; the first mattresses were piles of leaves, cornhusks, or other plant matter. Inventing textile techniques such as plaiting, weaving, and embroidery, some people developed sleeping mats that they placed directly on the ground, on raised surfaces, or on built-in extrusions of interior architecture. Others slept on rooftops, in hammocks, or in tents. But people of the preindustrial world measured safety and comfort differently from the way we do today: they often slept crowded with others, sometimes vulnerable to the elements.

Customs dictating when people sleep have varied over time and around the world, too. Roger Ekrich, in his 2005 book *At Day's Close: Night in Times Past,* argues

Figure 1
Robert Stivers (b. 1953),
Self-portrait in Water, 1991.
Silver gelatin print.

Figure 2
*Krishna and Balarama,
Watched Over by Nanda and
Yashoda, Who Fans Them to
Sleep,* Bilaspur, India,
c. 1725, detail.
Opaque watercolor and gold
on paper, 8 x 10¾ in.
(20.5 x 27.5 cm).
Private collection.

that before Thomas Edison invented the electric light bulb in 1879, people slept according to natural biorhythms. Western Europeans seem to have gone to "first sleep," "first nap," or "dead sleep"—*premier sommeil* in French, *primo sonno* in Italian—after nightfall for about four hours. They rose around midnight and went about their cooking, tending children, reading, or writing for a few hours. Returning to bed refreshed, couples engaged in sex and then fell into a second period of sleep until dawn. For the poor, first sleep was the perfect time to commit petty crimes, and for witches, it was a natural time to practice magic. The interval after first sleep was also the time to contemplate one's dreams, nightmares, and visions before relaxing into the "second sleep." In central Nigeria, Tiv people have been known to wake after midnight to engage in animated conversations with others in their hut.[1] According to a recent Gallup poll on bed habits commissioned by the Swedish furniture company IKEA, Malaysians slept least among people surveyed in twenty-seven countries—an average of six hours and thirty-six minutes per night—and had a lot of sex the remainder of the time.[2]

Beds, and all they conjure up, remain an appealing subject in cultural life around the globe *(fig. 2)*. Cribs and cradles, shielding newborns with their rigid surrounds and dangling amulets, symbolize not only safety but also innocence. Clinging to our "blankies" beyond the cradle stage, like Linus in the *Peanuts* cartoon strip, we literally carry some of those feelings of protection and comfort with us. Lullabies, stuffed animals and dolls, a favorite kitten or puppy, and bedtime stories coddle the young and all of us.

Literature abounds with references to beds as places of comfort, refuge, and allegory. A lot of sleeping and a lot of lovemaking goes on in ancient myths. In one of the best-known tales of Roman mythology, that of Cupid (love) and Psyche (the soul), a palatial bed is the site of Psyche's happiest moments. She dreads her days and looks forward only to bedtime. Betrothed to a man she is forbidden ever to see, Psyche is pampered and prepared for her wedding night in a beautiful, fabric-swathed bed. She receives her husband, Cupid, every night in a dark room, where they engage in conjugal bliss. Sworn never to try to see him in the light, she eventually succumbs to temptation, and he flees her forever.

The expression "Somebody's been sleeping in *my* bed" reminds us that some bedtime stories, especially those of the Brothers Grimm, are frightening and that the bed can also be a scary place for a child. He or she might use a flashlight to read in bed at night, snugly under the covers, but might still check under the bed for dragons, aliens, or the bogeyman.

In a more adult vein, Judeo-Christian scripture is rife with disturbing references to beds, including images in stories involving monstrous and tyrannical characters.[3] In the Talmud, the giant King Og slept on his "great iron bed" and provided Father Abraham with his huge long tooth for his famous ivory bed.[4] Afraid of going to sleep because of his nightmares, Job nonetheless said, "I have made my bed in the darkness." People lived in fear of having their beds literally pulled out from under them if they owed a debt, as when Solomon asked, "If thou hast nothing to pay, why should he take away thy bed from under thee?"[5] The Christian prayer "Now I lay me down to sleep; I pray the Lord my soul to keep; if I die before I wake, I pray the Lord my soul to take" is another reminder that the bed can be dangerous territory.

Navigating through the night with a good book of poetry is a way to soothe bedtime anxieties. Robert Louis Stevenson's collection of poems *A Child's Garden of Verses* includes the poignant "My Bed Is a Boat," in which the bedridden author tells us of his nocturnal activities "on board":

> At night I go on board and say
> > Good-night to all my friends on shore;
> I shut my eyes and sail away
> > And see and hear no more.
>
> And sometimes things to bed I take,
> > As prudent sailors do;
> Perhaps a slice of wedding cake,
> > Perhaps a toy or two.

The Princess and the Pea, Hans Christian Andersen's enchanting tale of a young girl who proves she is a true princess by her ability to feel a tiny pea through a special bed of twenty mattresses and duvets, reminds us that genuine beauty is inner sensitivity, not outer attractiveness. With characteristic humor and wisdom, the Tibetan Buddhist master Patrul Rinpoche commented on the modern Westerner's preoccupation with frivolous details of life such as redecorating hotel bedrooms:

> *Remember the example of an old cow,*
> *She's content to sleep in a barn.*
> *You have to eat, sleep, and shit—*
> *Beyond that is none of your business.*[6]

The realm of sleep and dreams has figured prominently in poetry since ancient times. It is evoked in this eloquent stanza by the twentieth-century poet Pablo Neruda:

> *Sometimes I sleep, I go back*
> *To the beginning, falling back in mid-air,*
> *Wafted along by my natural state*
> *As the sleepyhead of nature*
> *And in dreams I drift on,*
> *Waking at the feet of great stones.*[7]

Rainer Maria Rilke, whose writing often seems insurmountably enigmatic, created around the act of sleeping one of his most vivid and fluid passages in *Sonnets to Orpheus:*

> *Almost a girl it was and issued forth*
> *From this concordant joy of song and lyre,*
> *And clearly shining through her springtime veils*
> *She made herself a bed inside my ear.*
>
> *And slept in me. And all things were her sleep.*
> *The trees I marveled at, those*
> *Feelable distances, the meadow felt*
> *And every wondering that befell myself.*
>
> *She slept the world. You singing god, how*
> *Did you so perfect her that she did not crave*
> *First to be awake? See, she arose and slept.*[8]

"Bedded down in eternity" is the way the writer Gina Berrault described the plight of women in her short story "Women in Their Beds."[9] The dialogue among her female characters, who work in a hospital, centers on the bed, the place where women spend so much of their lives. The bed as object and word hovers over every scene. As the women tend patients at bedside and recall the significant beds in their own lives or reflect on life metaphorically—sometimes it is "a bed of thistles," sometimes a "bed of roses"—the novella is pervaded with beds.

The erotic nature of the bed is undeniable *(fig. 3)*. Considering that in addition to being a place to sleep, it was once the scene of birth and still is a site of procreation, lovemaking, general coziness, and indulgence—as well as of healing and, if one is fortunate, death—the bed is a most sensuous object. Death itself can be sexually charged: we have everything from the French phrase *la petite morte,* meaning sexual climax and the deep sleep that follows, to the sex appeal of vampires—the living dead—and other types of necrophilia. Wedding-night beds and honeymoon beds, sometimes equipped with mechanical parts and surrounded by mirrored walls and crystal chandeliers, usually are substantially cushioned, softly draped, and laden with ornate pillows several layers deep. We may purchase posture-supporting mattresses or sleep on tatami, but for most of us in the West, the ideal fantasy bed is an antique four-poster with canopy, silk sheets, and luxuriant bedding. Emily Dickinson's poem "Ample Make This Bed" is an exquisite testimony to such longings:

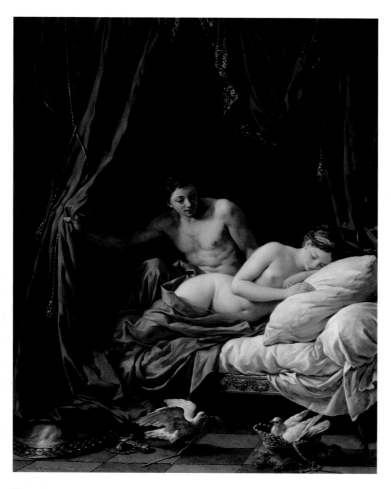

Figure 3
Louis Jean François Lagrenée
(1725–1805),
*Mars and Venus, Allegory of
Peace 1770.*
Oil on canvas,
25¼ x 21⅛ in.
(64.1 x 53.7 cm).
The J. Paul Getty Museum, Los
Angeles, 97.PA.65.

> *Ample make this bed.*
> *Make this bed with awe;*
> *In it wait till judgment break*
> *Excellent and fair.*
> *Be its mattress straight,*
> *Be its pillow round;*
> *Let no sunrise' yellow noise*
> *Interrupt this ground.*[10]

Artists use the bed as metaphor. Robert Rauschenberg's 1955 work *Bed (fig. 4)* can be seen as an intimate self-portrait, in that the bed frames an old pillow, a sheet, and what is purported to be one of the artist's own quilts. It is one of Rauschenberg's early "Combine" works, in which he combined painting with found objects; in this case he drew and splashed paint on the bedding and quilt and hung the artwork on the wall. Organized in this way, *Bed* offers the viewer a look at some of the most intimate objects of life in a disconcerting context. Placed vertically, this private object, usually seen obliquely in its normal horizontal position, is both literally and figuratively in our face. And how does this make us feel? Fifty years later, *Bed* is still a powerful artwork that elicits in us a slight uneasiness with our voyeuristic stance.

Conceptual art and political activism met in a 1982 exhibition called *Prisoners of Conscience,* organized by the Houston, Texas, chapter of Amnesty International. Artists were asked to design a bed for a particular political prisoner somewhere in the world. Assigned the Roman Catholic priest Father Calciu-Dumitreasa, imprisoned in Romania for speaking out against atheism, Mel Chin created an exceptionally evocative "bed" with a steel frame and headboard in the form of a cell gate and a Latin-cross-shaped mattress with spikes piercing the hand, heart, and feet areas. Elsewhere, addressing the issue of homelessness, Krzysztof Wodiczko, who since the late 1980s

has developed a series of instruments for homeless or immigrant operators that function as implements for survival, communication, empowerment, or healing, designed *Homeless Vehicle* (1988–1989), a motorized shopping cart cum artwork that served many purposes, including that of sleeping space.

Short-listed for the Tate Gallery's prestigious Turner Prize in 1999, Tracey Emin's installation *My Bed* is another type of bed as self-portrait. Strewn with rumpled white sheets, disheveled pillows, pantyhose, and a towel, a simple mattress on a platform is made sordid by the accompanying detritus on the floor and on the bed stand: condoms, contraceptives, cigarette packs, vodka bottles, and underwear. Accompanied by videos of the artist's home, the installation clearly mirrored her disheveled life.

Providing tension and mystery, a modern tubular bed with a net canopy is very much a third character in Eric Fischl's 2004 series of paintings, "Bedroom Scenes." Pared down to the essentials, close-ups focus on a middle-aged, upper-class husband and wife in various scenes of alienation, the bed literally and figuratively looming between them in its pristine, clinical whiteness.

In stark white and sinister black, the 2002–2005 installations *During Sleep,* by the Japanese artist Chiharu Shiota, aesthetically melded traditional Japanese textile art with avant-garde Japanese performance art, combining up to twenty beds encased in lacelike black webs. Viewing the empty beds as representative of the act of sleeping and dreaming of self and community, this artwork harked back to the fifth-century BCE Greek *asclepieion,* a public dream clinic.[11]

Inspired by "sleep, by the bed, by a dreamy state of reverie," the fall–winter 2005 collection by fashion designers Rolf Snoeren and Viktor Horsting featured elements taken from bedding. Some finely tailored outfits featured collars in the shape of pillows, but the pièce de résistance—or ridicule, according to one's point of view—was an ensemble in which a linen bedsheet dress was covered by a duvetlike coat featuring a soft-sculpture backsplash of two ornate silk pillows.

This book is about *real* beds *(fig. 5).* It offers a thematic history of humankind's design solutions to the need for a comfortable place to sleep. Not intending it to be encyclopedic, we instead chart some of the most common and most amazing of furniture and bedding, noting the significance of cultural mores, materials, and technologies. An exhaustive work about beds could be thousands of pages long, bound in many volumes. Pared down to the essentials, *Sleeping Around* nevertheless gives substantial information about topics that reflect its authors' areas of interest and expertise.

The book's chapters are organized around topics that reflect design styles, whether of court or country, and the premise that all beds and bedding are part of one global phenomenon: the need to sleep as well and in as comfortable and attractive a bed as possible. Whether looking at aristocratic beds from ancient Egypt, portable bedding from Turkey, or cutting-edge contemporary beds from Japan, our approach is that their purpose is fundamentally all the same. We hope readers will gain an appreciation for this most central and evocative object, the bed, while marveling at the remarkable diversity of its design across the globe. These objects belong to a single history of applied art, both literally and figuratively high and low.

Chapter 1, "Sleeping Low," shows how the low-platform, minimal beds that became fashionable in the West in the 1960s—and the Western hippie penchant for sleeping on a mattress on the floor—had their antecedents in Asian designs, as well as parallels in African societies *(fig. 6).* We may understand why servants in the Middle Ages slept on or near to the ground, but this chapter also describes courtly Ottoman sultans' penchant for sleeping low.

Figure 5
Vincent van Gogh
(1853–1890).
*La chambre de van Gogh à
Arles,* 1889, detail.
Oil on canvas,
22½ x 29¼ in. (57.5 x 74 cm).
Musée d'Orsay, Paris.

Cultural exchange and hybridization feature in the design of the beds and bed-ding discussed in chapter 2, "Sleeping High." Demonstrating again that many of the bed styles Westerners take for granted as being Western in origin appeared first in the East, I show how elaborate canopied beds emerged in Han dynasty China. Revealing influence in the opposite direction, some inventive hybrid four-posters in India—however different they may be in their intricate surface ornamentation—are nearly indistinguishable in form from their Georgian English equivalents.

The heavy, carved *lits clos,* or "closed beds," of Brittany, with decorations taken from Celtic designs, are among the odd and attractive beds described in chapter 3, "Sleeping in the Closet." Throughout France, even as far south as the Pyrenees, as well as in Scandinavia, the Netherlands, and Belgium, enclosing oneself in solid furniture shielded one from the chaos and burdens of life outside the cloistered environment of the cupboard bed.

Chapter 4, "Sleeping on the Move," describes the inventive way nomadic peoples have used textiles as beds and bedding in cultures where even the houses are made of soft materials, from tents to yurts. The information and images from Turkey are based chiefly on Bobbie Sumberg's own fieldwork. Rolled, piled, and placed on the ground is not the only way those who wander have designed their beds, and this chapter illuminates such marginalia as loft beds in the wagons of the Roma, or Gypsies, as well as the astounding artistic detail lavished on aristocratic *lits de campagne* and other traveling beds of the elites.

Figure 6
Ferdinando Scianna,
Youvarou.

Until recently, long journeys by train, ship, or airplane rarely provided a good night's sleep. Chapter 5, "Sleeping on the Road," offers a concise history of modern industrial design as it faced one of its greatest challenges—to create beds that were structurally sound and comfortable in a moving vehicle. Showing once more how different cultures and different strata of society, at different times in history, have created places for a good night's sleep, details about past and present notions of either basic or luxurious comfort pose the question of whether we are better off now.

The ways in which people view sleep, dreams, and beds today is informed by a rich multicultural vocabulary. Chapter 6, "Sleeping in the Modern World," opens with a discussion of the nineteenth-century health reform movement and its effects on bedroom and bed design. It then chronicles the history of beds in the twentieth and early twenty-first centuries. Heavily influenced by youth culture since the 1960s, Western designers of beds and bedding have drawn on ethnic fabrics and Eastern styles and customs. Sleep-deprived as many of us are nowadays, I end the chapter with a look at recent inventions for soothing our tired minds and bodies.

Does a baby sleeping close to its parent's heartbeat in a Snugli carrier feel more secure than one sleeping in a cradleboard? Does the gentle rocking of a cradle lull an infant to sleep more effectively than the sway of a simple rope hammock? In chapter 7, "Sleeping Small," Sumberg looks at the many types of small beds made to protect sleeping babies. She shows that cross-culturally and historically, people have devoted much attention to designing and embellishing beds and bedding for young children. Symbolic and heavily adorned, baby beds are fraught with talismanic and symbolic elements, their scale permitting lavish materials and decoration.

Ending the book, appropriately, is "Sleeping Forever . . . and Ever," chapter 8. Analogies between sleeping and death have flourished since ancient times. Edgar Allan Poe complained, "Sleep—those little slices of death, how I loathe them." Tomb art, from early to modern, has included images of sleeping, sometimes in beds; grave monuments and sarcophagi themselves have even been shaped as beds. The nefarious world of vampires, who sleep in coffins, reminds us that the coffin is usually our funerary bed, our final resting place. In the end, the bed as a symbol of life becomes a symbol of death, and for many, of the next life.

Notes

1. A. Roger Ekrich, *At Day's Close: Night in Times Past* (New York: W. W. Norton, 2005), 301–323.
2. *Nordstjernan* 132 (April 29, 2004): front page. The Gallup International Poll surveyed fourteen thousand IKEA customers in twenty-seven countries. The margin of error was 4.5 percentage points.
3. Jewish bed lore also includes auspicious beds, such as the *dargesh,* a low bed with leather strappings that served to bring good luck to the home and appease the "domestic genius." Reginald Reynolds, *Beds, with Many Noteworthy Instances of Lying On, Under or About Them* (London: Andre Deutsch, 1952), 73.
4. Ibid., 100.
5. Ibid., 70.
6. Sogyal Rinpoche, *The Tibetan Book of Living and Dying* (San Francisco: Harper, 1994), 20.
7. Pablo Neruda, *Stones of the Sky,* translated by James Nolan (Port Townsend, WA: Copper Canyon Press, 1987), 25.
8. Rainer Maria Rilke, *Sonnets to Orpheus,* translated by M. D. Herter Norton (New York: W. W. Norton, 1942), First Part, Sonnet 2, 19.
9. Gina Berrault, *Women in Their Beds: New and Selected Stories* (Washington, DC: Counterpoint, 1996).
10. Although this poem is probably about a gravesite, many think it is intentionally ambiguous or paradoxical. Sensually palpable, it remains evocative of any or every special bed in our lives.
11. Raphaela Platow, *DreamingNow* (Waltham, MA: Rose Art Museum of Brandeis University, 2005), 52.

1. Sleeping Low

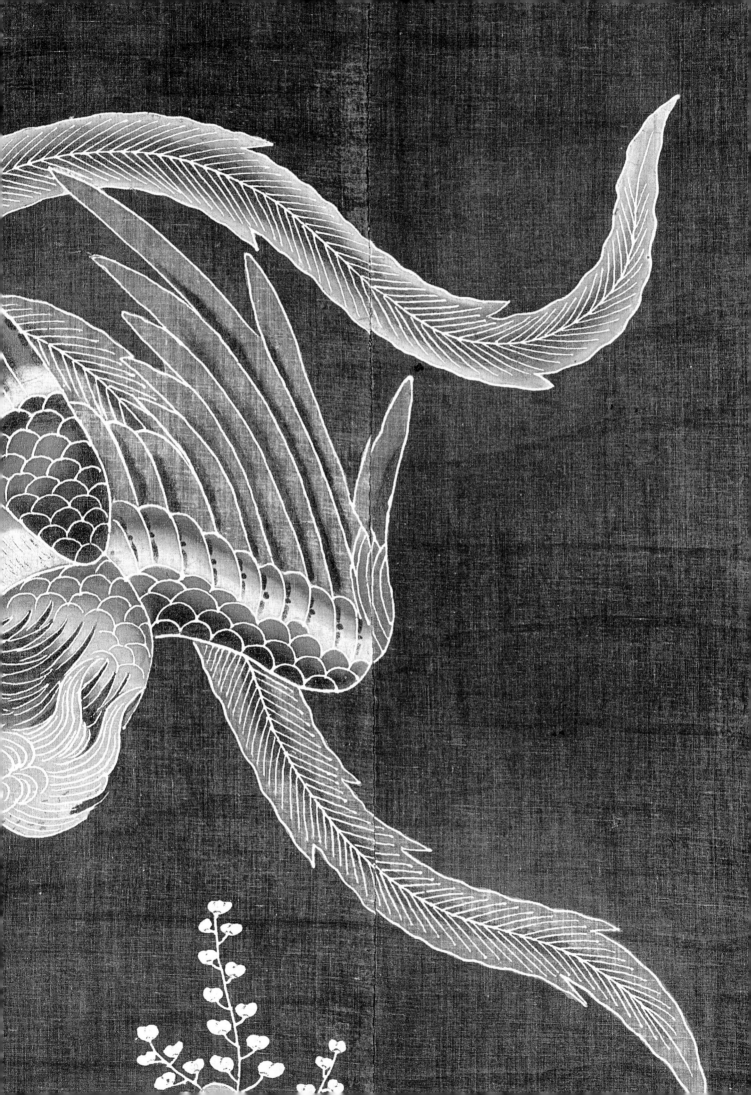

"Full moon on the tatami mats; shadows of the pine branches." —*Takerai Kikaku*

Bobbie Sumberg

Sleeping Low

Figure 7
Kimbei Kusakabe,
Girls in Bed Room, c. 1880.
Hand-colored albumen
photograph,
8 x 10 in. (20.3 x 25.4 cm).

Figure 8
Tsukioka Yoshitoshi,
*Prostitute Strolling by
Moonlight,* June 1887.
Ink on paper,
woodblock print,
14½ x 9 in. (36.8 x 22.9 cm).
Signed and inscribed: "Like reflec-
tions in the rice paddies: the faces
of streetwalkers in the darkness are
exposed by the autumn moonlight."
Museum of International Folk Art,
Else and Joseph Chapman
Collection.

Cultural attributes of sleeping develop from historical circumstance, religious belief, mythos, and environmental adaptation. In many parts of the world, floor is analogous to bed. Bed furniture is eschewed, and a mat or mattress is laid down for the sleeper's comfort. Sleeping on the floor in a house or building is not the same as sleeping on the ground in a tent; there is no obvious need for lightweight or portable bedding. Instead, this choice is based on other considerations—sometimes economics and status but also environment and cultural preference.

Historically in Europe, the closer to the floor one slept, the poorer one was. Servants and peasants slept on straw mattresses directly on the floor, while lords and ladies had elaborate beds with curtains and festoons. Cinderella, the unfortunate heroine of a folktale told all over Europe, slept on a pile of ashes she dragged from the fireplace to keep herself warm. The cinders not only supplied her nickname but also symbolized her loss of status when her father remarried. Her stepsisters had fine beds to sleep in.

In earliest colonial New England, the master and mistress of the house slept in a bedstead that folded during the day against the wall next to the kitchen fireplace, the only heat source in the log houses the colonists built.[1] The children slept upstairs in an unheated loft on pallets on the floor. With adulthood and marriage came the privilege of a bed. In many houses where space and means were limited, bedsteads were undoubtedly assigned on the basis of age and marital status.

Figure 9
Bedding cover *(futonji),*
Kyushu Island, Japan,
nineteenth century.
Cotton, painted pigments,
rice-paste resist *(tsutsugaki),*
65 x 51 in. (165.1 x 129.5 cm).
Museum of International Folk Art,
gift of Neutrogena Corporation.

Sleeping on the floor is a cultural and aesthetic choice for many people. Continental and island Asia offer a study in contradiction. Although furniture off the floor developed early in China—archaeological finds assumed to be the remains of raised platforms used as beds date from the thirteenth to the eleventh century BCE[2]—the use of furniture never took hold in other parts of the region. Although the Chinese migrated to many places throughout Asia and took their furniture habits with them, only the native inhabitants in the highest echelons of society used beds, tables, and chairs, usually for status purposes. A ruler needs a throne to raise him, literally, above his subjects, who live at floor level. The wealthiest members of a stratified society often adopt some of the material habits of outsiders who come either as merchants bringing new goods and ideas or as colonizers imposing a foreign way of life. The raised wood or iron bedstead found a limited audience in Asia, outside of China *(see fig. 49).*

Sleeping on the floor requires certain kinds of bedding. The best-known floor sleepers are the Japanese, and essential to understanding how and why the Japanese sleep on the floor is the tatami-futon ensemble *(fig. 7).* The origins of tatami can be traced back to the general use of woven sedge and other plant fibers for floor coverings that could be folded up and stacked in a corner when not in use. Indeed, the word *tatami* comes from the verb *tatamu,* which means "to fold."[3]

Tatami first appeared during the later Heian period (794–1185 CE), taking on the dual role of seating and bedding. Called *okitatami,* they were used as throw mats and spread around the room as the situation demanded. Similar to the tatami of today, they were rectangular with dimensions of about 70 by 35 inches (180 by 90 cm). Their shape and size, which is believed to have been based on the measurements of the human body, indicate that they were used for sleeping. Indeed, several paintings from this period depict people sleeping on *okitatami.*

The shift from *okitatami,* which were placed here and there in a room, to the tatami that completely covered the floor of the room began in the fifteenth-century homes of samurai. The modular and rectangular shape, with the length and width in a two-to-one ratio, led to a logical and convenient transition from scattered mats to entire floor covering. That the dimensions of the mat were expected to match those of the human body is reflected in an old Japanese saying, "Half a mat to stand, one mat to sleep" (*Tatte hanjo, nete ichijo*). This codified "bed shape" became a unit of standard measurement that determined the spatial configuration of most dwellings in Japan. Government housing statistics are still based on the number of tatami that make up the rooms in a house, although the actual dimensions attached to the mats have varied and grown smaller, especially since World War II.

Futon, the most commonly recognized type of Japanese bedding, did not come into common usage until the seventeenth century. Prior to that, most of the Japanese population slept on straw mats spread on the bare earth or on raised wood planks. They kept warm by covering up with the few simple work clothes in their possession. Even the pampered aristocracy lay directly on the floor, slumbering under layers of their gorgeous silk robes *(fig. 8)*.

The importation and successful cultivation of cotton in Japan in the sixteenth century revolutionized Japanese bedding.[4] Before that time, the staple fiber for commoners' clothing and other textiles was bast fiber, *asa*, a word that refers to a variety of different fibers. Although strong, these fibers not only required hours of labor-intensive cultivation and production but were also coarse and ineffective as insulation. Silk, which had been available in Japan since the third century CE, was too expensive for the majority of people. Cotton's relative ease of cultivation, affordability, and exceptional qualities of warmth and comfort meant that even the humblest Japanese villagers were able to enjoy sleeping on a mattress for the first time. In addition, cotton's ability to take dyes was superior to that of bast fiber textiles, so a new world of design and pattern became possible. Elaborate rice-paste resist *(tsutsugaki)* floral and figurative motifs, bold plaids and stripes, and intricate ikat *(kasuri)* pictures woven into a deep indigo ground enriched the visual environment of village homes across Japan. All of these decorative techniques were incorporated into bedding covers, which were then stuffed with wadded cotton *(fig. 9)*.

The term *futon* refers to a combination of two components: *shikibuton*, a plain-weave cotton mattress stuffed with cotton batting, which is placed directly on the tatami mat floor, and *kakebuton*, a thick, plain-weave cotton coverlet stuffed with cotton or feathers, with periodic stitches to keep the stuffing in place. Some of the most luxurious futon were made of silk and stuffed with silk floss. In more recent times, the *kakebuton* has often been covered with a white, fitted sheet for protection. The *yogi*, a variation of the *kakebuton*, or coverlet, developed during the Edo period (1603–1867). Similar in shape to a kimono, the *yogi* was constructed with an additional panel of fabric inserted in the center back and triangular gussets at the underarms to create extra room for sleeping *(fig. 10)*. Winter *yogi* were stuffed with cotton batting. After centuries in which the Japanese slept in their clothing, the *yogi* offered an intimate and practical connection between tradition and newfound comfort.

During the day, people aired their futon by spreading them on top of the hot ceramic tiles of lower-level roofs. Contemporary urban apartment dwellers hang their futon out over balconies and later put them away in built-in closets with sliding doors, called *oshiire*. In some traditional homes and travel inns, they are stored in large, deep, free-standing chests called *futon dansu*.

Traditional Japanese pillows *(makura)* were essentially light, wooden, rectangular boxes with either flat or convex tops and bottoms *(fig. 11)*. On the top was placed a small cylindrical cushion stuffed with buckwheat hulls. The cushion was tied to the box with a string, which also secured a sheet of soft folded paper, perched on the very top, which served as a pillowcase and was changed as necessary.

Figure 10
Bridal sleeping cover *(yogi)*,
western Japan, nineteenth
century.
Cotton, silk, rice-paste resist
(tsutsugaki), 64 x 62 in.
(163 x 157 cm) overall in a
closed position.
Museum of International Folk Art,
gift of Neutrogena Corporation.

Other materials for pillows included woven bamboo *(fig. 12)* and porcelain. Porcelain pillows could be filled with hot water in the winter and cool water in the summer. For the Japanese traveler, there were pillows that folded up and stowed away in a small circular box, within which were drawers and spaces for portable paper lanterns *(chōchin)* and toilet articles.[5] Pillows were designed not to cushion the head but to support the nape of the neck while the shoulder rested naturally on the floor. They also helped protect the elaborate coiffures of aristocrats, samurai, and courtesans. During the Meiji period (1868–1912), pillows developed into something more like the Western-style pillow, although they were smaller and still stuffed with buckwheat chaff or red beans.

In twenty-first-century Japan, traditional houses have been replaced by concrete high-rise apartment buildings in densely populated urban areas. Living spaces are still small, and the need for multipurpose rooms makes the use of portable bedding practical and even inescapable.

Sleeping mats laid directly on the floor or ground are used in other places in Asia as well. The Dayak people of Borneo make intricately patterned mats from rattan *(figs. 13 and 14)*. They use mats as floor coverings, for seating, and for sleeping in the longhouse, the traditional architecture of the rural Dayak. Although the longhouse structure varies with each Dayak group, the general arrangement is a series of rooms, each belonging to a family, connected by a long veranda. The interior living space is divided into a common area for cooking and eating and a sleeping area that is separated from the common area by walls.

Figure 11
Headrests, Japan, c. 1950.
Lacquered wood base with
cylindrical pillow wrapped in
paper on top of base; at base
7⅞ x 6¼ in. (19.5 x 16 cm)
and 7⅞ x 6¾ in. (19.5 x 17 cm).
Museum of International Folk Art,
IFAF collection.

Figure 12
Headrest, China, c. 1950.
Bamboo, plaited,
4½ x 12½ x 5¼ in.
(11.4 x 31.7 x 13.3 cm).
Museum of International Folk Art,
gift of the Girard Foundation.

Each person living in a longhouse has a sleeping mat.[6] The mats are made by women, who split the stem of the rotan palm to make a pliable strip that is then plaited. Leaves from the *Pandanus* palm are used for a softer, less durable mat. No loom is

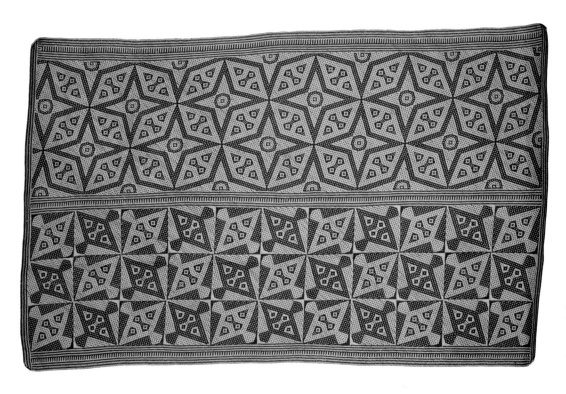

Figure 13
Mat, Borneo, c. 1970
Rattan, dye, plaited,
36 x 59 in.
(91.4 x 149.8 cm).
Museum of International Folk Art,
gift of Lloyd Cotsen and
Neutrogena Corporation.

Figure 14
Mat, Borneo, c. 1930
Rattan, dye, plaited,
71 x 40 in.
(180.3 x 101.6 cm).
Museum of International Folk Art,
gift of Lloyd Cotsen and
Neutrogena Corporation.

Figure 15
Sleeping mat. Vietnam. c.1925.
Cotton. woven.
71½ x 40½ in.
(181.6 x 102.8 cm).
Museum of International Folk Art.
IFAF collection.

employed. Mat weavers create designs by using materials of different colors derived either from natural variations in the plants or from dyes.[7] Manipulating variations of key and diamond shapes, they form abstracted representations of living creatures such as centipedes, snakes, and birds. Versions of these two basic forms serve as borders and bands. The same motifs appear on baskets, weavings, and the human body as tattoos. Mats with elaborate designs of human figures, houses, and the tree of life are not for sleeping but are used in rituals.[8] In Vietnam, weavers interlace indigo and white cotton into elaborate patterns of snakes and ancestor figures *(fig. 15)*. Householders then use the cloth as a sleeping and sitting surface in the house.

In Turkey, where most furniture was unknown until the mid-nineteenth century, even the Ottoman sultans had no beds. Domestic architecture in Turkey grew out of the nomadic yurt, a wooden lattice frame covered by felt with a domed top (see chapter 4). Yurt and tent dwellers used textiles for both sleeping surfaces and coverings.

As the Turks settled and built houses, the habit of portable bedding remained with them, along with the spatial concept of the tent. In traditional Turkish houses the rooms connect not with each other but with a central open space called the *sofa*. The arrangement of rooms around the *sofa* clearly recalls the arrangement of tents in a family group around an open, courtyardlike space. Low platforms called *sedir*, constructed around the perimeter of the room, echo the use of cushions to sit on and storage bags to lean against lining the back wall of the tent *(see fig. 70)*. Although to the casual eye the *sedir* might look like furniture, structurally it is a section of the floor that has been raised a few inches. Built-in cupboards to hold bedding and other household items are the major departure from the soft furnishings of the nomad.[9]

Figure 16
Hiroshi Mochizuki,
Hirota Guest House
Kyoto, Japan.

Figure 17
Mat, Great Lakes region,
Ojibwa people, c. 1880.
Basswood, reed, vegetable dye,
29 x 57 in. (71 x 139 cm).
Museum of International Folk Art,
gift of Lloyd Cotsen and Neutrogena
Corporation.

Even in the supreme opulence and luxury of Istanbul's Topkapı Palace, started by Sultan Mehmed II in the mid-fifteenth century and continually enlarged and occupied until the mid-nineteenth century, beds, chairs, and tables did not exist. The last Ottoman rulers, however, in the mid-nineteenth and early twentieth centuries, took increased interest in European ways and built new palaces along the Bosporus, furnished in the European style. Until then, the Ottoman sultans living in the Topkapı Saray slept in a fashion similar to that of the Anatolian city dweller, villager, and nomad. Undoubtedly their rugs and pads were of better quality than those of the commoners, but the principle was the same. Sleep could happen anywhere that bedding could be laid down.

One aesthetic dimension of sleeping on the floor relies on simplicity, the serenity of the nearly empty room. Textiles, whether woven of rattan, cotton, or silk, dominate the visual environment. The angles and hard edges of wood or metal furniture give way to the rounded, padded corners and surfaces of pillows, cushions, quilts, and pads. Yoshida Kenko (1283–c. 1350), essayist and poet, expounded on the Japanese aesthetic of artful minimalism in 1330: "A house which multitudes of workmen have polished with every care, where strange and rare Chinese and Japanese furnishings are displayed, and even the bushes and trees of the garden have been trained unnaturally, is ugly to look at and most depressing. How could anyone live for long in such a place?"[10] At the opposite end of the spectrum, the tiled rooms of a Turkish palace, filled with patterned pile rugs, figured velvet cushions, and embroidered wall hangings and incidentals, are as lively and visually overwhelming as any bedroom crowded with a canopied bed, draperies, and upholstered furnishings. Sleeping low is not universally correlated with the aesthetic of simplicity.

Sleeping on the floor is not always simply a matter of convenience or poverty. Religious mendicants, whether wandering Buddhist or Franciscan monks, choose to sleep rough in accordance with their belief in the spiritual richness of poverty. Developing a close relationship with one's natural surroundings and the gods who reside there is a fundamental principle of Japanese religious belief. For the Japanese, sleeping on the floor brings one closer to the experience of the *yamabushi,* an ascetic who lives in the mountains and resides in the axis connecting heaven and earth. The *yamabushi* cultivates a Buddha nature by undergoing many hardships, including sleeping on the ground with nothing more than a thin mat.[11] By sleeping on the floor, the ordinary person acts like the more spiritually enlightened *yamabushi,* thus reinforcing his or her religious belief. Traditional Japanese rural inns, now catering to harried urbanites seeking respite from the city, still allow guests to experience the tranquillity and beauty of communion with nature *(fig. 16).*

Figure 18
Headrests, Ethiopia, c. 1950.
Wood, beads; *left to right:*
5½ x 5½ in. (14 x 14 cm),
6½ x 6½ in. (16.5 x 16.5 cm),
6¼ x 6⅝ in. (15.8 x 16.7 cm).
Museum of International Folk Art, anonymous gift.

Figure 19
Pillow, *(both sides shown),*
Gansu area, China,
2500–2000 BCE.
Jade,
2½ (center) x 3¾ (base) in.
(6.35 x 9.5 cm).
Private collection of Spencer
Throckmorton.

Figure 20
Bed. *Dameria*, Spain. 2005.

Sleeping low has never been limited to Asia. Native Americans plaited mats from local plant materials for sitting and sleeping on *(fig. 17)*, as did many peoples in Africa and Latin America. The use of headrests or hard pillows was widespread on the African continent *(fig. 18)*, in continental Asia, and along the Pacific Rim. Neck rests of many forms and materials, such as carved wood, stone, and basketry, though uncomfortable-looking to the contemporary eye, have provided comfort and ease to sleepers for centuries. Jade pillows *(fig. 19)* are still used by an elite few who claim that the coolness of the stone soothes the tired mind.[12]

Today, the practice of sleeping low has survived in few places except as an economic necessity or an adaptation to climate. Modern village houses in Côte d'Ivoire, for example, are built of concrete block with tin roofs. They are nearly uninhabitable during the hot-season nights, when windows are closed for security and to keep out mosquitoes. The inhabitants of such a house with a bedstead in the bedroom often sleep on a mat in the courtyard, where any breeze cools the night air. Plastic mats suffice until rain or a need for privacy intervenes.

The spareness of decoration and the functional simplicity of some modern design from the 1950s to the present translates the aesthetic of simplicity to the present day. That aesthetic does not limit one strictly to a simple mat on the floor; a low platform bed without a headboard or footboard can also effectively create a haven of peace in a visually overburdened world *(fig. 20)*.

Notes

1. Alice Morse Earle, *Home Life in Colonial Days* [1898] (Stockbridge, MA: Berkshire Traveller Press, 1974), 55.
2. Sarah Handler, *Austere Luminosity of Chinese Classical Furniture* (Berkeley: University of California Press, 2001), 105.
3. Atsushi Ueda, *The Inner Harmony of the Japanese House* (Tokyo: Kodansha, 1990), 80.
4. Reiko Mochinga Brandon, *Country Textiles of Japan: The Art of Tsutsugaki* (New York: John Weatherhill, 1986), 38–40.
5. Edward S. Morse, *Japanese Homes and Their Surroundings* (Tokyo: Charles E. Tuttle, 1972).
6. Charles Hose and William McDougall, *The Pagan Tribes of Borneo*, 2 vols. (London: Macmillan, 1912), p. 41 of ebook read online at www.gutenberg.org.
7. Carla Zainie, *Handcraft in Sarawak* (n.p.: Borneo Literature Bureau, 1969), 8.
8. Bernard Sellato, personal communication, 2005.
9. Önder Küçükerman, *Turkish House: In Search of Spatial Identity*, 5th ed. (Istanbul: Touring and Automobile Association of Turkey, 1996), 148–149.
10. Yoshida Kenko, *Essays in Idleness*, translated by Donald Keene (New York: Columbia University Press, 1967), 10.
11. Hitoshi Miyake, *Shugendo: Essays on the Structure of Japanese Folk Religion*, ed. H. Byron Earhart (Ann Arbor: University of Michigan Press, 2001).
12. Ellen Tien, *New York Times*, August 25, 2002, Section 9, p. 11.

Annie Carlano

Sleeping High

Raising themselves off the ground on which most people of the world slept, whether directly or buffered by straw, textiles, or mats, certain ancient civilizations, in far corners of the world, developed designs that English speakers know as bedsteads, more commonly called beds. Made of wood, marble, bronze, and other durable materials, from the very beginning such furniture was adorned with textiles, both practical and luxurious. As we will see, the bed as furniture is inextricable from the varied and elaborate fabrics that, increasingly throughout time, covered, concealed, and decorated the solid architectural framework.

The first beds were simple raised platforms, elevated above the damp and drafty floors. The more exalted the sleeper, the taller the platform, an overt symbol of high rank and the celestial realm. Pictorial representations of deities in China depict them seated on platforms of exaggerated height, to underscore their divinity. The oldest archaeological evidence of raised platform furniture from China consists of marble and bronze pedestals dating to the Anyang period of the Shang dynasty, from the thirteenth

Figure 21
Episode from Stories of Filial Piety, detail
(side of a stone sarcophagus).
Northern Wei Dynasty
(386–534 CE), China.
Engraved limestone.
24½ x 88 in. (62.2 x 223.5 cm).
The Nelson-Atkins Museum of Art,
Kansas City, Missouri
(Purchase: Nelson Trust). 33-1543/1.

Figure 22
Bed of Queen Hetepheres I
(reproduction), Egyptian, Old
Kingdom, Fourth Dynasty,
reign of Snefru to Khufu,
2582–2575 BCE.
Wood, gold, copper, silver,
leather, faience, ebony,
17⅛ x 38⅜ x 69¹¹⁄₁₆ in.
(43.5 x 97.5 x 177 cm).
Museum of Fine Arts, Boston.

to the eleventh century BCE.[1] Shaped in rectangular or square forms, such early furniture served several functions, from seating furniture by day to surfaces for erotic play and sleeping at night *(fig. 21)*. Indeed, as the bed form developed in China, it never lost its essential role as a place for more than one daily activity. There was no distinct "day bed" like that which developed in the Western world. The couch bed, with a railing on three sides and sometimes a higher back, is not to be confused with the modern Western sofa bed, although it may have inspired some of the latter's designs *(see fig. 93)*.

Even earlier evidence of beds comes from the late prehistoric era in Egypt (known there as the Predynastic period), around 3100 BCE. Known from archaeological finds and tomb paintings, these beds consisted of two long poles joined by shorter cross members at the head and foot *(fig. 22)*. The sides have holes or mortises for rope or rawhide webbing that would have supported a mattress, sheet, or blanket. The beds

were supported by short rectangular legs of ivory or wood— the only elements of the bed to be clearly exposed—which were sometimes elaborately carved with motifs of animal hooves or paws. Lightweight for portability, and with a footrest and headrest but no bed head, this was the design that inspired the form of the ancient Greek couch *(fig. 23)*.

To the ancient Greeks, the word *kline* designated a bed that, like the ancient Chinese equivalent, served as a platform for diverse activities. The Romans used primarily the word *lectus* for "bed," although Latin had more specific terms, too, such as *lectus scubicularis* for a bed on which to sleep, *lectus triclinaris* for a bed on which to eat, *lectus lucubratorius* for a working bed, *lectus sperulatus* for a bed on castors for the sick, and even *lectus gyrgatus* for a bed used for bound lunatics.[2] Leading scholars have shown that the Romans' bed functions were commonly interchangeable, so these names suggest the later Roman tendency toward excess rather than any exclusivity of usage.[3]

Like its Egyptian prototype, the ancient Greek and Roman bed was a narrow rectangle in its basic form, long enough for a person to stretch out on. The bed's legs, one at each corner, were taller than those of Egyptian beds, because the surface needed to serve as a dining table as well as a sleeping place, and they were rectangular or turned, almost a rule in the Roman world. The bed had no footboard but did feature a headboard to lean against while reclining. Stretched across the frame were interlaced straps of leather or flax, upon which rested a mattress. Although no bed cords have survived, they are mentioned in ancient literature. For example, in Aristophanes' *Lysistrata,* produced in 410 BCE, Myrrhina says to Kinesias, who refuses to have a mattress on his bed, "It is nasty to lie on the bed cords."[4]

Greek ideas about home furnishings reached the Etruscans by the sixth century BCE. Etruscan beds, created in the basic rectangular shape with feet, were of a robust massiveness, with squat feet, a very low footboard, and a higher headboard—as so beautifully portrayed in the famous "Sarcophagus of the Married Couple" from the Banditaccia necropolis of Cerveteri, Italy.

A removable canopy supported by posts sometimes augmented fine ancient platform beds. Remarkably, several of these have survived. Dating from the height of

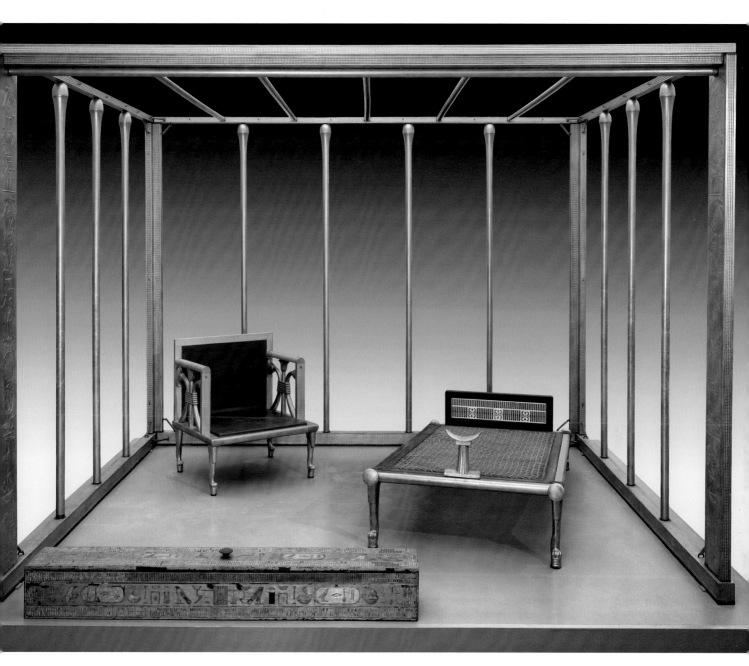

Figure 24
Furniture from the tomb of
Queen Hetepheres I
(reproduction). Egyptian.
Old Kingdom. Fourth
Dynasty, reign of Snefru to
Khufu, 2582–2575 BCE.
Wood, gold, copper,
silver, leather, faience, ebony.
Museum of Fine Arts, Boston.

the "pyramid age" in Fourth Dynasty Egypt (c. 2625–2500 BCE), the tomb of Queen Hetepheres I contained a bed lavishly embellished with gold foil, along with its detachable canopy *(fig. 24)*. The collapsible rectangular framework of gilded wood poles would have held a piece of fine linen to act as mosquito netting. When not in use, the curtains were stored in a long box covered with semiprecious stones, underscoring the importance of such textiles. Two beds from the fourth century BCE were found in a tomb at Baoshanin Jingmen, Hubei province, China. Designed entirely in parts to be assembled and disassembled, they are not unlike furniture one finds today in Hong Kong's antique stores, where it is stored flat or shipped in its various parts.[5]

An illustration after Gu Kaizhi (c. 344–406), from "The Admonitions of the Instructress to the Court Ladies," shows an early example of a Chinese canopy bed in a domestic rather than a ceremonial scene *(fig. 25)*. A platform with four posts supports fabric that surrounds the bed to create a room within a room. Sometimes such canopy beds had six posts, in which case the curtains were hung on the inside of the bedstead.[6]

Sleeping surrounded by cloth was partly an attempt to cope with environmental factors such as cold and insects, but it also lent privacy at a time when people had no special chambers designated exclusively for sleeping, so that families and servants slept close together.[7] In the ancient world the bed was the largest and most spectacular piece of furniture in the home, and its portability allowed the splendor to be taken out of doors. In China the predilection for flat sleeping surfaces persisted, whereas in the West people developed a desire to sleep on an incline. But the basic design solution for providing furniture in which to work, play, eat, and sleep remained the same: platform, legs, posts, and canopy.

The ancients used luxurious textiles to decorate their beds. The Chinese, who discovered silk and were, by the Shang period, capable of weaving intricate twills, and who developed the principle of the draw loom before the Han dynasty (206 BCE–220 CE), created legendary bed hangings. Prized possessions, they were of silk, often embroidered with auspicious symbols such as flying immortals. A poem by Wang Song from the time of the Han dynasty gives poignant testimony to the symbolic meaning of bed curtains to wife betrayed:

Figure 25
The Canopy Bed, woodblock illustration from Min Qiji's 1640 edition of *The Story of the Western Wing (Xixiang ji),* leaf 13. Museum für Ostasiatische Kunst, Cologne, inventory no. R 61,2 (no. 13).

Figure 26
Fresco, Casa del Centario, Pompeii, Italy.

Your curtain is flapping before the bed!
I strung you there to screen us from daylight.
When I left my father's house I took you with me.
Now I take you back.
I will fold you neatly and lay you flat in your box.
Curtain, will I ever take you out again?[8]

In ancient Egypt, bed hangings and bedding were usually of fine linen and sometimes wool, and bedspreads could be of luxurious leopard fur, such as that on the bed from the Old Kingdom tomb of Nefer and Khay.[9] Animal skins were also used in the Greek world. For example, a wealthy prince from Cyprus in the time of Alexander the Great lay on a couch covered with a "smooth carpet." Bedcovers of linen or wool, expensive materials, and even gold threads, with patterns of animals or stars, were described as "delicate," "well-woven," and "glistening."[10]

In both East and West, pillows were part of the bed accessories. What is fascinating is the great dissimilarity in people's choices of materials and sizes. Early Chinese, Egyptian, and Nubian pillows (like later African and Japanese ones) were conceived as small pieces of furniture composed of rigid materials, designed with a dip to cradle the head (see ch. 1).[11] It is often said that this custom resulted from a need to protect complicated hairdos. Greeks (who did use head rests early on but then evolved headboards), Etruscans, and Romans—those arbiters of conspicuous consumption—preferred soft pillows on which to rest their heads and bodies *(fig. 26)*. Why such radical differences?

Figure 27
Joseph's Dream,
southern Italy (Salerno-
Amalfi), 1050–1100.
Ivory,
6½ x 4¾ in. (16.5 x 12 cm).
Victoria & Albert Museum, London.

The Chinese platform was large enough to sit on comfortably in traditional poses while entertaining, working, or reading, whereas the Greeks and particularly the Romans needed to be propped up and "cushioned" on their narrower beds for quotidian social activities. It is also possible that remaining still while sleeping was the ideal in China, whereas the Greeks and Romans considered active tossing and turning, with a larger part of the body cradled, to be the norm.

From early medieval Europe we have less rich a repository of extant furniture or pictorial images of beds. The seventh-century CE royal burial at Sutton Hoo, England, yielded the earliest find of bed hangings in northern Europe, but not until the eleventh century do we find not only depictions of beds in sculpture and paintings (chiefly in manuscripts) but also the beginning of a literature about beds, from inventory lists and early dictionaries to works of nonfiction and fiction.

Around the year 1000, the bed in Europe retained the basic shape of the Egyptian-derived Greco-Roman form, which had spread throughout the Roman Empire. The predilection for a sloped surface, higher at the head end, continued. Early Norwegian "great beds" had staggered planks across the bottom, rather than ropes, to support their mattresses. They had mortar-and-tenon joins and head posts taller than their footboards, carved with fanciful animal heads not unlike those seen in the bed of King Edward as depicted in the so-called Bayeux Tapestry, dated around 1082.[12]

Indeed, changes in the design of beds took place slowly. The lathe-turned legs earlier favored by the Romans, for example, are clearly indicated in an eleventh-century bed seen in a southern Italian ivory carving that is thought to show the Old Testament story of Joseph's second dream. In the scene as depicted in Byzantine works, the sleeping Joseph rests under a coverlet and is propped up by a substantial bolster, creating the desired inclined sleeping position *(fig. 27)*.

Beds become larger in Europe in the twelfth century. In France they are known to have been as long as about 13 feet and as wide as 11½ feet (4 by 3.5 m). Beds stood high enough off the ground that objects such as urinals and small chests could be conveniently stored underneath them. Such great surface areas required servants to use long sticks *(bâtons de lit)* to smooth out the sheets and bedcovers *(fig. 28)*. The increased size and prominence of the bed in France corresponded to an expansion of bed terminology. A *lit complet* consisted of a wood frame, the *châlit,* in beech or oak, decorated with a bottom of wooden planks. Several terms applied to low beds with wooden wheels that could easily be moved from room to room: *couchette roulonee, châlit roulenez,* and *couchette roulenesse.* The simpler cord or tied bed was called the *châlit corde.*[13] The designation *chambre à coucher* (bed room) did not appear until the mid-thirteenth century.

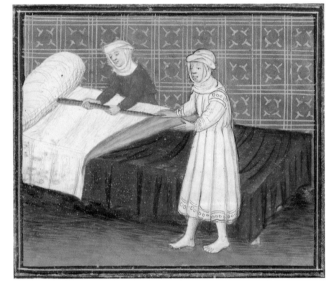

Figure 28
Guillaume de Digulleville.
Roman des trois pèlerinages.
fourteenth century.
Bibliothèque Nationale de
France.

By 1250, the basic elements of a "good bed" were the bedstead, the bottom mattress (called *une paillasse* in French because it was a big sack full of straw [*paille*] or leaves), and, on top of it, the proper mattress (*matelas,* from the Arabic *matrah,* meaning something thrown on the ground), made of linen or wool. A feather bed, called a *couste, coute, coite,* or *coquette,* was placed on top of the proper mattress and covered with a bedsheet of linen or hemp—the *drap,* the same word used in France today. Supporting the sleeper's head was the bolster, known as a *traverslit* (*traversin* today) because it stretched from one edge of the bed to the other. Pillows, cushions, or both went on top of the bolster. Such cushions were originally designed for use on seating furniture—chairs and benches—to give comfort to people's thighs and derrieres. The word *cushion* itself has a fascinating etymology that indicates that its origin lies in the Latin *coax,* meaning thigh. The German *kissen* (cushion) also means *hanche,* or thigh. Such pillows often doubled as sachets containing potpourris of sandalwood and other spices from Asia to impart a sensual scent to the bedding.[14]

Figure 29
Bed quilt, detail,
The History of Tristan, c. 1380.
White linen with cotton filling.
Victoria & Albert Museum, London.

Covering this multilayered bed was either a fabric coverlet (*couvre lit*), sometimes lined with fur, or a quilt (*courtepointe*). The latter word is from the Latin *culcita puncta*, indicating a needle-worked fabric with a soft inner core as insulation. The earliest extant bed quilts come from Sicily and date to about 1380 *(fig. 29)*.[15]

Bed shapes in the fourteenth century continued to evolve from earlier models. The Western predilection for elevating the upper part of the body and accentuating a downward slope to the feet resulted in two things: the use of more pillows on top of the bolster and the development of a prominent bed head *(fig. 30)*. For comfort and fashion, the hung bed, essentially a bed in two disconnected parts hung from the ceiling, with textiles suspended from the ceiling rafters and behind the bed head in an alcove, was in vogue in northern Europe and in Venice, in various regional designs, until about 1500. The French king Charles V (c. 1375) favored the canopy, of which there were three types: that which covered the entire length of the bed (the *celure*), that which covered only the top half of the bed (the *demi-celure*), and the smaller, conical "sparver," which in the fifteenth century became popular elsewhere—for example, at the court of Henry V and among some Florentine aristocrats.[16]

The standard form of the bed in Florence and central Italy from about 1300 to 1500 was the *lettiera (fig. 31)*. Architectural in its solidity and mass, it featured a tall headboard placed against the wall, usually topped by a deep shelf. Benches or chests stood against three sides of the bed, sometimes along with footboards. The bed looked like a giant platform or proscenium in the middle of a room, where it functioned as both a private and a social center. Householders could store their precious belongings, including clothes, in the chests of this multipurpose piece of furniture, then take them out and sit on the chests to facilitate dressing. Friends could sit on the benches when visiting, and the benches were also useful as tabletops for washbasins and food snacks.[17]

Canopy (*padiglione,* or tent) beds in Florence were first created by means of a cone-shaped or domed cap that hung by a cord attached to a hook in the ceiling. Curtains fixed to its lower edge spread out to encircle the bed below *(fig. 31)*. Placed above the bed head and middle of the bed, this type of canopy had the nickname *spaviero,* or sparrowhawk, because of the precarious way it hovered and swayed at the slightest touch. Servants were required to open and close the suspended bed curtain, and this inconvenience led to another approach, known elsewhere in the Middle Ages, of suspending the curtains on rings slipped over rods forming a square hung above the bed, or along a wall with a niche, in the ancient manner.

Northern Renaissance design solutions to suspending a canopy were feats of engineering. Through an elaborate system of cords whose orchestration also required the assistance of servants, wealthy homeowners pulled meters and meters of sumptuous fabrics into large, hanging, teardrop shapes to create a magnificent display of architecture and textiles during the day *(fig. 32)*. The design of such bed hangings—luxurious in their fullness, supple draping, and detailed construction—seems to have been focused on the shape of the hanging teardrop rather than on the pattern of the fabric.

Figure 31
Francesco Granacci.
Scenes from the Life of Saint John the Baptist, c. 1510,
detail.
Oil, tempera, and gold on
wood.
31½ x 60 in. (80 x 152.4 cm).

Metropolitan Museum of Art:
Gwynne Andrews, Harris Brisbane
Dick, Dodge, Fletcher, and Rogers
Funds, funds from various donors,
Ella Morris de Peyster Gift, Mrs.
Donald Oenslager Gift, and gifts in
memory of Robert Lehman, 1970
(1970.134.1).

Figure 32
Rogier van der Weyden,
Annunciation, c. 1460.
Alte Pinakothek, Munich.

Preference was for outside bed hangings in more modest, solid colors, rather than for the figured silks favored by the French, Italians, and Spaniards.

Yet given the flourishing textile trade at the time, and the presence of Florentine silk merchants in the Flemish world, it was not unusual to see a precious Italian brocaded velvet, one of the most expensive items of its day, used as a headboard, dominating the sleeping chamber when the curtains were drawn. Keeping warm was a top priority in cold, damp climates such as that of Flanders and the Netherlands—hence the heavy bed hangings that, when lowered, surrounded and insulated the sleeper.

Renaissance bed design in Venice was an anomaly. Drawing on central Italian, French, northern European, and Asian influences, beds there were unique. Two distinct types appeared in later fifteenth-century homes. One was the built-in bed (fig. 33). Mentioned in inventories and depicted in paintings, these beds were built into the wall—"fixed in the room in the Venetian fashion"—and were considered part of the architecture rather than furniture.[18] With no bedstead, it was textiles that truly defined the bed, from mattresses of down, wool, and cotton to opulent silk damask draperies, usually in green or red, along with lace-trimmed sheets and abundant cushions with gold-embroidered borders—all at a time when such textiles were as costly as silver and gold.

Figure 33
Vittore Carpaccio,
The Birth of the Virgin, 1504.
Oil on canvas,
49 x 50 in. (126 x 129 cm)
Academia Carrara, Bergamo, Italy.

The other prevalent type of bed was the gilded iron bedstead, sometimes on wheels and with a canopy (*da pavion*) suspended from the ceiling. By the end of the century the canopy was squarish and hung on a tester actually attached to the bedstead by posts (fig. 34), sometimes detachable. The metal bedstead was described as a camp bed (*una corruola da campo*).[19]

Beds with posts seem to have developed in Venice by the third quarter of the fifteenth century, possibly first in the form of a portable traveling bed.[20] What is clear is that both stable and mobile forms of post-and-rail construction became widespread in the sixteenth century. With a post at each corner, the design now permitted the canopy to be attached to the bed itself, so that curtains and valances could be managed with greater ease. Sometimes, particularly in northern Europe, the canopy or tester was made of solid wood, with intricate carving replacing opulent fabrics (fig. 35). Artists and architects became interested in applying their talents to the design of these new posted beds, seeing the posts as opportunities to create decorative sculptural columns. It was not unusual in Italy to find posts with capitals and testers treated as entablatures. The style in classically oriented Florence was for plain lathe-turned and painted posts, known as "alla Toscana" both then and today *(fig. 36).*[21]

Adorning the Tuscan four-post bed, known as a *cuccia,*[22] was a variety of coverlets *(copriletti),* usually conceived of separately from the bed hangings. The topmost layer of the bedding was so luxurious that it was ultimately forbidden by sumptuary laws. Beyond the highly coveted woven silk fabrics, the Florentines used wool and silk tapestries as coverlets. Just as the Flemish imported Florentine silks, so the Florentines imported prestigious tapestries from Flanders, as well as fine linen sheets. Italians customarily slept with the coverlet on the bed—it was not a mere decorative accessory—which may be why the outermost layer was sometimes a heavy, tapestry-woven coverlet, a quilt, or a layer of one of various types of pile. These "hairy" bed-covers are depicted in paintings and were known as *bernia,* from Hibernia, because they were thought to have come from Ireland. Not unlike a Greek *floccati* or a Finnish *ryijy*—which I will come to shortly—they were the faux fur fabrics of their day.[23]

Rome in the high Renaissance was considered the most beautiful city in Europe, and most of the greatest artists of the day worked there on papal and aristocratic family projects. Not surprisingly, then, the bed design that became the standard for the next two centuries was created in Rome. In comparison with the more linear and graceful form that had appeared in Venice and Florence only a decade or so earlier, the Roman version was more like a small building, a massive tour de force of furniture and decoration that commanded the room. Depicted in a 1511 fresco by Sodoma in the Palazzo della Farnesina, the bed shown in figure 37 was possibly designed by the Sienese architect Peruzzi.[24] Carved or painted with mythological and biblical allusions, such beds reminded viewers of the owner's majesty and godliness, as in the example of the bed of Pope Urban VIII, from the Palazzo Barberini, now at Caramoor in upstate New York. The balance and regularity of the room's interior take their cues from the bed itself.

Perfection of the technology of turning hard materials on a lathe, coupled with imperial Rome's earlier predilection for spooled legs on beds, led to the imaginative designs of turned columns in sixteenth-century Rome *(fig. 38)*—popular decorative ele-

Figure 35
The Great Bed of Ware,
c. 1590.
Oak, carved and originally
painted, with panels of
marquetry; modern textile
hangings.
Victoria & Albert Museum, London.

Figure 36
Bed *alla Toscana*,
fifteenth century. Palazzo
Davanzati, Florence, Italy.

ments on subsequent exuberant baroque models as well. In the seventeenth century and into the eighteenth, Spanish and particularly Portuguese beds also featured splendid lathe-turned details *(fig. 39)*. With more finely turned columns, thinner than those on Roman beds of the time, these beds boasted spiraling details that were not confined to the corner posts but were added to the headboard, footboard, or both as decorative elements, creating an airy, openwork quality not unlike that of the fashionable needle lace of the day.

In the early decades of the seventeenth century, France surpassed Italy as the innovator and trendsetter in all interior decoration, including bed styles. Although beds from 1680 to 1715 got very tall, the actual form of the bedstead did not change. Reigning as a state or ceremonial bed, or *lit de parade*, head against the wall, the enormous posted bed was often protected by a balustrade. Bedding and bed hangings became increasingly opulent and exotic, the result of technical advancements and the opening of new trade routes. These new, fresh textiles became the organizing theme of the home's interior, and in the bedchamber it was the bed hangings with which all other furnishing fabrics had to harmonize.

Brought to France by Catherine and later Marie de Médicis, Italian silk weavers, embroiderers, and lace makers invigorated the textile industries there. Some of the greatest decorators were now creating designs for damasks and velvets with the grotesque and arabesque ornaments made fashionable at Fontainebleau, where François I and his daughter-in-law, Catherine de Médicis, brought the Italian style to court. Marie de Médicis married Henri IV in 1600, and by 1606 the number of court embroiderers had more than doubled. Their status rose, too: they now occupied the best apartments in the Louvre.[25] Lyon replaced the cities of Italy as the center of the silk-weaving industry, and the perfection of the draw loom there around 1606 permitted shades of colors to be used in silks that rendered motifs more naturalistic.

Figure 37
Il Sodoma,
*Wedding of Alexander the
Great and Roxanne*, c. 1511.
Fresco. Palazzo della
Farnesina, Rome, Italy.

The bed was the preeminent showcase for these exquisite new fabrics, and the art of the upholsterer became a prestigious profession. Damasks and velvets gave way to sophisticated, colorful compositions influenced by Charles Le Brun, director of the Manufacture Royale des Meubles de la Couronne, and, at the end of the century, to lace-patterned silks *(fig. 40)* and exuberant floral motifs in the Bizarre style. Conceived en suite, window treatments, wall coverings, and the upholstery of seating furniture lent uniformity and a feeling of being swathed in luxury. Indeed, in 1692 it was said in France that the mark of a good courtier was that he was a master at tying elaborate bed curtains.[26] This new way of living, in an interior both comfortable and beautiful, was to become the paradigm for most of Europe.

Silks were not the only fabrics being used in fashionable interiors. Imported painted and dyed cottons from India made their way to English and Dutch ports on ships of the East India Company and to Marseille on those of the *Compagnie des*

Figure 38
Giovanni Battista Montano,
*Sketches of Six Columns for
Important Beds*, c. 1600.
Sir John Soane's Museum, London.

Figure 39
Portuguese spindle-turned
bed, eighteenth century.
Victoria & Albert Museum, London.

Indes, until they were regulated and ultimately banned toward the mid-eighteenth century. Produced specifically for the European market, these "oriental," colorfast textiles for both dress and furnishings were quickly coveted. For the bed, hangings and palampores (from *palang-posh,* meaning bedcover) were even more desired than silk fabrics, until the secrets of their manufacture became known and imitated *(fig. 41).* In France, a major industry sprang up, at first merely copying but eventually developing its own *indiennes* printed designs in centers such as Marseille, Jouy-en-Josas, Nantes, and Alsace *(fig. 42).* In Britain, the tree-of-life pattern of many palampores was a major influence on eighteenth-century crewelwork bed hangings *(fig. 43).*[27]

Daniel Marot (1663–1752) was the first designer to create purely "French" compositions, free of the prevailing Italian styles. Epitomizing the baroque style, his compositions, consisting of large-scale, repeated botanical motifs enclosed by fluid strapwork "frames," were elegant expressions of French classical taste *(fig. 44).* A Huguenot, Marot left France for the Netherlands a year before the revocation of the edict of Nantes in 1685 to work for the Stadtholder, later William III. There, where his engravings after the French style were circulated, his great influence was in disseminating the concept of a room designed as a whole. While he worked in England in 1694–1698, his designs became more restrained, responding to the Palladian style of Inigo Jones and others in vogue at the time, as can be seen in the bed he created for the English country house Dyrham Park in 1704.

When a more fanciful interior design emerged around 1720, as the rococo style developed in France and spread throughout continental Europe, the actual shapes of rooms changed. They became more organic, with rounded corners, coved ceilings, and, in the case of private apartments, niches in walls, sometimes containing beds. A sliding wall incorporated at the back of the niche might enable servants to make the bed more easily.[28]

Now covered with silk weavings in more intricate, delightful, even whimsical patterns in a lighter palette, the bed sparkled in its surroundings of pastel-colored decorative paneling, mirrors, and lots of candlelight. During this time, the designs of furnishing fabrics changed often and embodied a range of virtuoso techniques, from brocaded silks with wrapped silver and gold threads to warp-printed *chiné* and other Asian-inspired stuffs.

English interiors, furniture, and beds around the middle of the eighteenth century reflected different aesthetics, never straying far from the harmony of Palladian principles as interpreted by Robert Adam and William Kent. Other decorative schemes and designs favored Chinese and even Gothic motifs. Thomas Chippendale's publications and designs, such as the bedstead in the Chinese style shown in figure 45, exemplify the rococo in England.

By the 1770s, French bed designs had proliferated. Clever variations of forms created in the Middle Ages and Renaissance, styles were renamed or embellished, and keeping the terminology straight is a challenge. The *lit en pavillon,* a bed with a conical

Figure 40
Chasuble front, c. 1725, detail. Silk, so-called lampas liseré, weft patterned with supplementary patterning wefts, 14½ x 27½ in. (36.83 x 69.85 cm). Wadsworth Atheneum Museum of Art, Hartford, Connecticut. Purchased with funds from the Florence Paull Berger Fund.

Figure 41
Palampore, made in India for the European market, mid-eighteenth century. Drawn and painted cotton backed with European woodblock-printed cotton, quilted, 78 x 94 in. (198.1 x 238.8 cm). Reverse side detail shown below. Museum of International Folk Art, gift of Paul and Elissa Cahn, MNM Art Acquisition Fund, Barbara H. Lidral Estate Bequest, Connie Thrasher Jaquith, Folk Art Committee, Textile Gift Fund.

or semicircular tester suspended from the ceiling, was still in use and was sometimes called the *lit en dôme*.[29] The *lit à la duchesse* (with a canopy that ran the entire length of the bed), although it existed in the Middle Ages as the *lit à plein ciel* or the *lit à épervier*, appeared under that name at the very end of the seventeenth century and was also known as the *lit à chapelle* and the *lit à la française*. According to Peter Thornton, the *lit à la française* was the four-post bed, the *lit à colonnes*.[30] To confuse matters further, the *lit à piquets*, a bed with a headboard and two low foot posts, was also referred to at least once as a *lit à la française*, in a 1772 print by Roubo.

The great state or ceremonial bed that I mentioned earlier as the *lit de parade* was a style known in the late Middle Ages and Renaissance as the *lit de parement* and *lit d'honneur*. Household servants slept in a *lit de domestique*, which was alternatively called *lit de valet de ferme, lit de serviteur, lit de veille,* and *lit de vacher*.[31] Referring to foreign tastes, certain bed designs, such as the *lit à la turque* (or *à la sultane*), *lit à la romaine,* and the extravagant *lit à la polonaise*, were beds placed against a wall with a dome-shaped canopy or tester.

Neoclassical bed designs (1770–1820) featured models dictated by Napoleon to

Figure 42
Bed *à la duchesse*, Munster, Alsace, France, Hartman & Fils, 1800–1810. Cotton, wood-block printed, 73 x 51 in. (182.5 x 127.5 cm). Private collection.

Figure 43
Crewel bed hangings from the Lennoxlove Set, probably Scottish, c. 1720. Dimity embroidered with wool and silk, each curtain 99 x 94 in. (251.5 x 238.8 cm), valance 10.5 x 216 in. (26.7 x 548.6 cm). Private collection.

Figure 44
Large textile fragment, France, c. 1720, detail. Silk, metal, and chenille embroidery, silk satin-weave ground. 43 x 150 in. (109 x 381 cm). Wadsworth Atheneum Museum of Art, Hartford, Connecticut. Costume and Textile Purchase Fund.

Figure 45
Japanned black and gold bed in the Chinese style, probably made by Chippendale, English, c. 1755. Victoria & Albert Museum, London.

create a national style inspired by ancient prototypes. Beds that had much more exposed furniture, with "ancient" Egyptian, Pompeian, or Etruscan elements such as swan legs and ormolu decoration, received names such as *lit à la romaine antique, lit mi-egyptien,* and *lit bateau,* or *lit gondole.*

Around the same time, Thomas Jefferson brought his knowledge of French furniture traditions to the bed he designed for himself for his home, Monticello *(fig. 46)*. In what was perhaps the most creative bedroom of its day, he adapted the basic raised platform on legs, surmounted by layers of mattresses, by placing it—in brazen modernity—in the space created by a pierced wall, so that its occupant could enter and exit from either of two rooms.

Most beds and bedding in the American colonies, however, were in the Dutch or English style, and a unique type of bedcover appeared in the Connecticut River valley *(fig. 47)*. Its strong design of floral blossoms with curving vines was accomplished by the unprecedented technique of cutting looped running stitches to make the pile.

In colonial inventories the terms *rugge* and *rugg* refer to this bedcover.[32] Not unlike the faux fur coverlets mentioned earlier, these heavy bedcovers were particularly useful in cold, damp climates. They differed in the extraordinary artistic attention lavished on their making and in the significance they held for the young women who made, signed, and dated them, as well as for the families who cherished and preserved them.

Bed design in England in the first half of the nineteenth century diverged from that in France and the rest of continental Europe. Whereas Napoleon proclaimed a national style called "empire," its grandiosity culled from ancient kings and emperors, English designs were created by architects, gentleman scholars, and reformers, chiefly for members of the upper class, not for royalty. That said, certain aspects of French style coexisted in England, particularly the Egyptianesque, although it seems to have stemmed as much from Nelson's victory in the Battle of the Nile as from any other influence. Other styles, such as Regency chinoiserie, were unique to England.

Rooted in intellectual and scientific concerns, furniture books by Thomas Hope and George Smith in the first decade of the century expounded the importance of designs of beauty, character, and meaning—in Hope's case—and robust, massive, even designs—in Smith's case—prefiguring the tenets of the social reformer and artist William Morris. In the late 1820s and the 1830s, Augustus Welby Northmore Pugin was designing Gothic-style furniture. Fired by a fervent Catholicism, his interests in furniture and the spiritual fused to produce masterworks of medieval-inspired furniture, including beds. Beginning in the 1830s, in Europe and the colonies, beds, like all other seating and sleeping furniture, became overupholstered and covered in heavy, neo-Renaissance hangings. These consisted of industrially produced textiles demonstrating a "holocaust of craftsmanship" and leading to a series of artistic revolutions, from aestheticism to modernism.[33]

In premodern Europe, most people in major urban centers slept in simplified versions of aristocratic and upper-class bed styles. This was not always precisely the case for residents of rural and provincial Europe and other parts of the world. In some places, for logical or mysterious reasons, intriguing solutions to bed design cropped up. Revealing attitudes about both art and culture, these beds and their textiles represent a meritorious history parallel to that of mainstream European sleeping furniture. Fascinating bed forms and noteworthy bedding have been made all over the world, from

Figure 46
Thomas Jefferson bed, Monticello, Virginia, eighteenth century.
Thomas Jefferson Foundation, Inc.

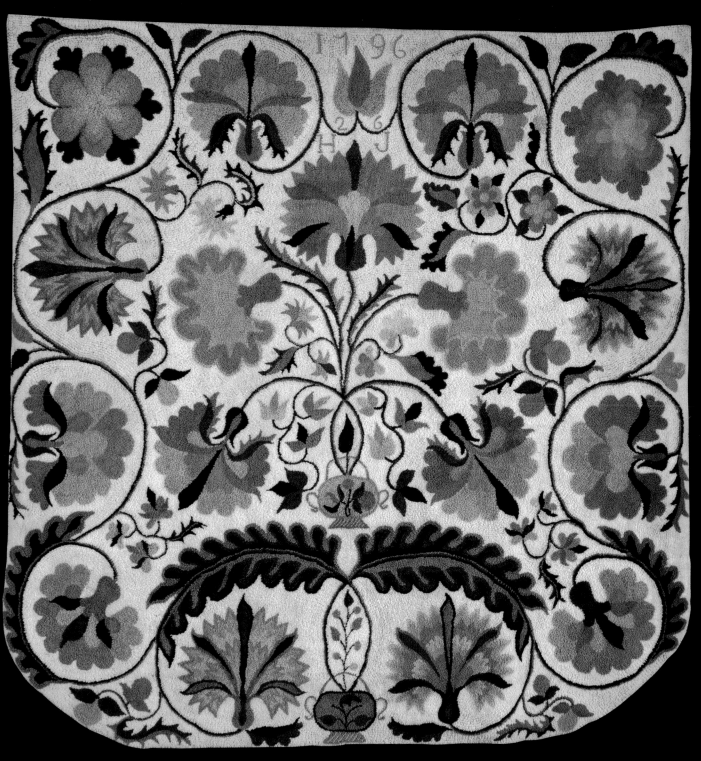

Figure 47
Hannah Johnson (1770–1848),
bedcover ("bed rugg"),
New London County,
Connecticut, 1796.
Wool, plain weave, embroi-
dered with wool yarns in
looped running stitches, cut to
form pile.
98¼ x 97 in. (249.9 x 246.1 cm).
The Art Institute of Chicago,
Restricted gift of the Needlework and
Textile Guild of Chicago, 1944.27.

Figure 48
Four-post bed,
Kerala, South India, mid-
nineteenth century.
Lacquered wood, red and
polychrome,
82 x 84 x 46 in.
(208.5 x 213.5 x 117 cm).
Collection Joss Graham.

the piled-high mattresses and pillows of the Princess-and-the-Pea type in eastern Europe to the handsome low wood beds and plaited beds of the Middle East.

The traditional Chinese couch bed and canopy bed influenced the basic forms of Indian sleeping furniture. Consisting of a wooden platform with four short legs, a rail along three sides, four tall posts, and a canopy, the nineteenth-century bed shown in figure 48 was not so distant in its conception from its Chinese antecedents. The turned details, painted surface, and hand carving are typical of a regional style that developed, displaying Western and specifically British features in the inclusion of a headboard and footboard and in the graduated shaping of the posts. Earlier Indian beds could be very low to the ground *(see fig. 2)*, but the platform and canopy were even then desirable, and pillows placed at each end of the bed accommodated the head and the feet.

The same ancient Chinese designs—platform bed, couch bed, and canopy bed—were reflected in the beds of certain parts of Indonesia where immigrants from mainland China settled and introduced the styles they knew. Displaying a harmonious blend of immigrant and indigenous traits, a bed from the village of Madura, Java, is shown in figure 49. Occupying the rail frieze and feet of the bed are intricate low-relief carvings of Javanese flowers and volutes in a free and fluid style. Above them, at the front, rectangular panels feature more rigid botanical ornamentation inspired by traditional Chinese carving. Pineapple motifs incorporated into the Chinese decoration are symbols of the island of Madura, where the fruit grows in abundance. Preserving the original function of the sleeping surface, this wooden platform was covered with a simple woven mat. Other Sino-Indonesian beds have caned platforms and different details, but the basic form of the bed is the same.[34]

Figure 49
Bed, Madura, Java, c. 1920.
Teak, paint,
93½ x 85½ x 60 in.
(239.7 x 219.2 x 153.8 cm).
Museum of International Folk Art,
IFAF collection.

The Neapolitan family bed, also known as a wedding bed, was a type of nineteenth-century iron-and-brass bedstead with a headboard and footboard connected by rails *(fig. 50)*. Because the history of this bed is shrouded in legend, because it was relatively unimportant in mainstream Italian culture, and, perhaps most of all, because a bed is a very private object to most Italians, information about its origin is absent in the literature about Italian regional furniture and folklore.[35] Some oral traditions say that in Campania, the region of which Naples is the capital, poor families used these beds in their communal sleeping room for the entire family. Others mention that people traditionally gave such beds to couples as wedding gifts.

Whatever their past, these historic beds have become sought-after pieces of "country" furniture throughout Italy and have spawned many fine reproduction workshops, even as far away as France *(fig. 51)*. Their special charm lies in their painted inserts, which depict, for example, regional seascapes, alluring young women in fancy eighteenth-century dress, and even the eruption of Mount Vesuvius. The former owner of the bed shown in figure 50, Giorgio Flores, wrote this poem about his feelings for it:

Figure 50
Bed, Campania, Italy, c. 1880s.
Iron, brass, paint,
64½ x 80 x 69 in.
(163.8 x 203.2 x 175.3 cm).
Museum of International Folk Art,
IFAF collection.

Figure 51
Contemporary wrought iron
bed with painted inserts,
Empoli, Tuscany, Italy.
Private collection.

"Vesuvius and My Bed"

On elaborate designs by artisans of old
*   By dint of hammer blows*
And skilled wringing of red hot metal
*   Unknown blacksmiths*
Built my bed.
And to reduce the effect of blows
*   And heat and anxious toil*
A gentle hand above my head
*   Painted the picture*
Of a quietly dormant
*   Gentle Vesuvius.*

The character of Vesuvius has been compared to
that of the Neapolitan people, so famous for their
bonhomie, patience, and philanthropic philosophy,
yet ready to blow up into fierce revolts—and just as
quickly to forgive and forget.[36] Its sexual connota-
tions also make Vesuvius a most provocative image
with which to adorn a bed.

Traditional Provençal beds, or *litoches,* are
made of local walnut, with tall headboards and shorter footboards, cabriole legs, and carved symbols
of the region. Arlésiennes dressed in traditional costume, sheaths of wheat, olive and oak tree branches, and almond tree sprigs are typically depicted on
beds of the region. A spectacular bed of this type,
now in the collection of the Museon Arlaten, was
designed by Léo Lelée for the *préfet,* or presiding
government official, Dautresme, in 1932 *(fig. 52).*
The artist revived the traditions of earlier centuries
to honor both this distinguished man and the city
of Arles.[37]

Frederic Mistral, the Nobel-Prize-winning
poet and leader of the *félibrige* literary movement
(1850–1950), wanting to restore Provençal language
and preserve traditional art and culture, amassed a
large collection of objects, including furniture, that he
acquired from families in the villages and countryside
of Provence. Among the cradles he found,
some show the work of the finest cabinetmakers
and carvers, whereas others display the simpler yet
ingenious design solutions of fishermen and
shepherds.

The blankets and coverlets used with these
cradles were of cotton and linen. The most prestigious type was the *boutis,* a whitework or solid-col-
ored textile. It consisted of two pieces of fine
linen or cotton sewn together, a meandering vine

Figure 54
Door of bed tent,
Kos, Dodecanese islands,
Greece, sixteenth century.
Linen embroidered with
colored silks and silver-gilt
thread,
98¾ x 20 in. (251 x 51 cm).
Victoria & Albert Museum, London.

and Provençal symbols drawn onto the cloth, and a length of candlewick or fine cord inserted with a needle into the pattern. Unique to southern Provence and the adjoining Langue d'Oc, this technique originated in medieval quilts used in the western Mediterranean during the fourteenth and early fifteenth centuries. The delicate, small-scale patterns dictated by the very fine wick required much time to create, and for this reason most extant *boutis* work takes the form of children's clothes and coverlets. Large bedcovers are rare; they were usually made for special occasions such as marriages, major political events, and high religious ceremonies. Featuring a pomegranate motif, the meticulously stitched bedcover shown in figure 53 was possibly made as a wedding gift, since pomegranates are associated with fecundity.

Demonstrating the intersection of East and West, court and country, the wedding bed tents of the Greek Dodecanese islands, in the Aegean Sea off the coast of Turkey, display unusual and lavishly embroidered designs. Known since the Byzantine era for their "beautiful silk needlework, . . . mainly bed tents," people of the Dodecanese produced textiles that remain collectible and valued today.[38] The bed tent doorway shown in figure 54, worked in lustrous silks and silver gilt-wrapped threads on finely woven linen, illustrates the highest quality of workmanship. Mimicking the carved stone gateways of the Dodecanese, the gable of this wedding tent panel is a cloth entranceway into the nuptial chamber.[39] The bed tent was the artistic center of the home, brightening the mostly dark and gloomy interiors of the small island houses.[40] It hung from a conical disk suspended from the ceiling and surrounded a bed placed in the middle of the floor as the room's focal point, in the style of the medieval European canopy bed.

Figure 55
Bedcover, Epirus, Ionian islands, Greece, eighteenth century.
Linen, silk,
66 x 96 in. (168 x 244 cm).
Museum of International Folk Art, gift of Lloyd Cotsen Family and Neutrogena Corporation.

The bed tent panel shown in figure 54, from the island of Kos, is embroidered in polychrome in a fine single darning stitch. It includes a repeating pattern of flowering plants, stags, and birds, with a narrow geometric border worked in red silk. Above these elements is a pattern of stylized human figures, some with bows and arrows, along with lions, leopards, stags, double-headed eagles, parrots and smaller birds, floral stems, and ships. Bed tent masterworks of this type are thought to have been made in professional workshops rather than in homes. Supporting this theory is the fact that the panel pictured in figure 54 is known to have belonged to the Platanislas family, one of the oldest and most respected on Kos.[41]

Wedding bedcovers from the Ionian island of Epirus are particularly alluring in their iconography, which reflects the predominant influence of the Balkan countries *(fig. 55)*. Decorated with male figures thought to be the groom, the father of the bride, and male attendants, along with birds and tulips and carnations in vases, these bedcovers were made by young women as part of their dowries.

Domestic embroideries throughout the Greek islands were made to be treasured but mainly to be used. Fragile textiles wear out, and bed hangings and bedcovers in their original state are rare. For centuries women have saved cherished remnants and sewn them together to form piecework bedcovers such as the carefully assembled example shown in figure 56.

Figure 56
Piecework bedcover, Greek
islands, assembled in the
nineteenth century.
Linen, silk,
71 x 96½ in. (183 x 245 cm).
Museum of International Folk Art,
gift of Lloyd Cotsen Family and
Neutrogena Corporation.

A heavy, long-pile type of bedcover known as the *ryijy* has been among the
most cherished of household textiles in Finland since the late Middle Ages *(fig. 57)*.
Early examples, known to us from inventories and other writings, were first mentioned
at a convent at Vadstena in 1451, and shortly thereafter their use was documented in
Norway (where the type was called the *ryer*). Used in Swedish castles from the early
sixteenth century (and known there as the *rya*), this textile eventually developed as a
floor rather than a wall covering. It became fashionable throughout the Western world in
the 1960s and 1970s. It is the historic Finnish *ryijy,* however, that is known throughout
historic Scandinavia as the most aesthetically pleasing of all.[42]

Displaying a surface quality similar to that of the New England bed rug, the *ryijy*
has a pile made not by needlework looping but by introducing looped knots between
the warps at regular intervals during the weaving and then cutting them, in the manner
of oriental carpets. It seems that in the earliest *ryijy* the pile faced down on the bed,
probably to give greater warmth to the bed's occupants. Occasionally the pile was dou-

Figure 57
Bedcover or rug *(ryijy)*, tulip
design. Finland, c. 1800.
Linen, wool.
70 x 53½ in. (178 x 136 cm).
Museum of International Folk Art.
IFAF collection.

Figure 58
Bedcover or rug *(ryijy)*,
geometric design, Finland,
mid-nineteenth century.
Linen, wool,
82 x 60 in. (208 x 152.4 cm).
Museum of International Folk Art,
gift of Lloyd Cotsen and
Neutrogena Corporation.

ble faced, ensuring even greater warmth. Most *ryijy*, however, were made with the pile facing up.

Their designs were at first solid natural colors, with a dominant yellow. Patterns of floral and geometric motifs have been studied and categorized from extant works of the eighteenth to the mid-nineteenth century in private and public Finnish collections, including those owned by the great Finnish expatriate designer Eliel Saarinen.[43] Drawing inspiration from Finnish sampler motifs, the running vine or garland borders and tulips in vases, with characteristically Gustavian stripes, indicate a late-eighteenth- or early-nineteenth-century date for the *ryijy* seen in figure 57. The reductive geometric composition—a central field of one color—and zigzag border of the *ryijy* in figure 58 are typical weavings made at the end of the historic period, around 1850.[44]

Valued by Finnish society in its heyday, the *ryijy* was both an important form of practical applied art and a symbolic object. It has been written that Finnish brides and grooms stood on this type of textile during their wedding ceremony. Included in a bride's dowry, the *ryijy* belonged to the wife after the death of her husband and continued to be used for the "widow's bed."[45] Whereas in most parts of Finland and Scandinavia the *ryijy* was used in conjunction with other types of bedcovers—furs, woven coverlets, heavy blankets—in at least one area of Finland, the Aland Islands, the *ryijy* was the only bedcover used.[46]

Finnish design has been characterized by its "purity and function." Gradually, around 1900, the function of the *ryijy* changed from that of bedcover to rug or wall hanging.[47] But for many citizens the historic bedcovers became emblematic of Finland's rich cultural traditions, as expressed in the 1918 exhibition *Suomalaisia ryijyjä* (Finnish *ryijy*) and in the government-sponsored research and publication of U. T. Sirelius's 1924 book, *The Finnish Ryijy*.[48] Finns continued to use such textiles on beds in the home into the modern era. These versatile *ryijy* were at the same time on the floor as rugs, on the walls as "art," and on beds, keeping people warm.

Notes

1. Sarah Handler, *Austere Luminosity of Chinese Classical Furniture* (Berkeley: University of California Press, 2001), 105.
2. Information from the *Acta Sanctorum* as cited in Reginald Reynolds, *Beds, with Many Noteworthy Instances of Lying On, Under, or About Them* (London: Andre Deutsch, 1952), 73.
3. Kim J. Hartswick, "The Greek and Roman Bed" (unpublished manuscript, 2004), 2–3; Florence Dupont, "Des chambres avant la chambre," in *Rêves d'alcôves: La chambre au cours des siècles* (Paris: Union Centrale des Arts Décoratifs and Reunion des Musées Nationaux, 1995), 13–14.
4. Hartswick, "Greek and Roman Bed," 3.
5. Handler, *Austere Luminosity*, 139–140.
6. Ibid., 142.
7. In the later Roman period, there were separate rooms for sleeping. See Pascal Dibie, *Ethnologie de la chambre à coucher* (Paris: Editions Métailié, 2000), 44–47.
8. Handler, *Austere Luminosity*, 143.
9. Peter Lacovara, "Beds in Ancient Egypt and Nubia" (unpublished manuscript, 2004), 4.
10. Hartswick, "Greek and Roman Bed," 4.
11. In Egypt, some pillows have been found wrapped with padding, but they are still rigid. Lacovara, "Beds in Ancient Egypt," 1.
12. Norwegian beds continued to be ingeniously shaped and carved, as well as painted, into the nineteenth century. See Janice S. Stewart, *The Folk Arts of Norway* (New York: Dover, 1972), 24–50. Information about the beds depicted in the Bayeux embroidery is from David M. Wilson, *The Bayeux Tapestry* (New York: Knopf, 1985), 218–219.
13. Dibie, *"La domestication de la chambre à coucher,"* in *Rêves d'alcôves*, 25–28; Dibie, *Ethnologie*, 71–72.
14. Dibie, *Ethnologie*, 72–73.
15. One is in the collection of the Bargello National Museum in Florence; the other is in the collection of the Victoria and Albert Museum, London. In October 2004 I was fortunate to examine the Bargello quilt at the Opificio della Pietra Dura national conservation lab at the Fortezza da Basso, Florence, with Susanna Conti, director of the Textile Technical Section, Paola Cesari, consulting textile conservator, and Mirella Stragapede from the University of Bari who was writing a thesis on the quilts. Given the physical evidence and the fact that there are multiple quilts, the possibility that these textiles were originally created

as wall hangings or banners to mark a marriage, rather than as bed quilts, is under study. Costume and other visual details suggest a slightly later date than 1380. It is hoped that a focused study of both quilts will be published in the near future.

16. Edward Lucie-Smith, *Furniture: A Concise History* (London: Thames and Hudson, 1993), 47.

17. Peter Thornton, *The Italian Renaissance Interior, 1400–1600* (New York: Abrams, 1991), 114. An exhibition and book on this topic was being co-organized by the Arts and Humanities Board Center for the Study of the Domestic Interior, Royal College of Art, and the Victoria and Albert Museum, for autumn 2006.

18. Patricia Fortini Brown, *Private Lives in Renaissance Venice: Art, Architecture, and the Family* (New Haven, CT: Yale University Press, 2004), 77.

19. Ibid.

20. The portable *lit de camp* was first mentioned in 1472. It is possible that the form was from the greater Veneto. Peter Thornton noted that the form was referred to in a Roman inventory as a type found in France and Germany, and he asked whether those places might have been where the form originated. See Thornton, *Italian Renaissance Interior*, 144–145.

21. Renato de Fusco, *Storia dell'arredamento* (Torino, Italy: UTET, 1993).

22. Thornton, *Italian Renaissance Interior*, 141.

23. Ibid., 162.

24. Ibid., 139.

25. Annie Carlano, "Embroidery," in *French Textiles from the Middle Ages to the Second Empire* (Hartford, CT: Wadsworth Atheneum, 1986), 88–89.

26. Peter Thornton, *Authentic Décor: The Domestic Interior, 1620–1920* (London: Seven Dials, 1993), 58. The term *lit d'ange* is the seventeenth-century renaming of the medieval and Renaissance *lit à demi ciel*. See Nicole de Reynies, *Le mobilier domestique vocabulaire typologique*, vol. 1 (Paris: Imprimerie National, 1992), 230.

27. For information about the palampore, see Ruth Barnes, Steven Cohen, and Rosemary Crill, *Trade, Temple and Court: Indian Textiles from the Tapi Collection* (Mumbai: India Book House, 2002), 22.

28. Thornton, *Authentic Décor*, 94.

29. Reynies, *Mobilier domestique*, 254.

30. Peter Thornton, *Seventeenth-Century Interior Decoration in England, France, and Holland* (New Haven, CT: Yale University Press, 1983), 160.

31. Reynies, *Mobilier domestique*, 210–255.

32. *Bed Ruggs 1722–1833*, exhibition catalog (Hartford, CT: Wadsworth Atheneum, 1972).

33. Lucie-Smith, *Furniture*, 136.

34. Information from Lori Ostlund and Anne Raeff, formerly of the gallery Two Serious Ladies, Albuquerque, New Mexico.

35. See Salvatore Settis, *Il classico nel futuro* (Torino, Italy: Einaudi, 2004). Thanks to Marisa Iora, cultural anthropologist at the Museo Nazionale delle Arti e Tradizioni Popolari, Rome, and Francesco Ramella, Professor of Sociology, University of Urbino, as well as members of the Flores family for their comments on the Neapolitan bed in Italian culture.

36. Letter from Giorgio Flores, 2 October 2004. I thank Heidi Flores and Lorenzo Balloni for their assistance with the acquisition of this Neapolitan bed by the Museum of International Folk Art, and to the entire Flores family for their interest in this project and assistance with my research. Metal beds have been associated with Sicily and Campania since the late eighteenth century, not just for hygienic reasons but due to regional craft traditions. See Piero Pinto, *Il mobile italiano dal XV al XIX secolo* (Novara, Italy: Istituto Geografico de Agostini, 1962), 150, and Roberto Pane, *Costumi e scene popolari di Napoli* (Naples, Italy: Grimaldi, 1994), 13, concerning the tradition of the *scuola di Posillipo* landscape painting that influenced popular imagery.

37. I thank the staff of the Museon Arlaten for their kind assistance with my research on the Provençal bed and its textiles while I studied there in May 2004. Director Dominique Serena-Allier granted me carte blanche access to the collections, library, and archives at a time of inconvenience for many of the staff. I am grateful to them all for their cheerful assistance.

38. Susan L. MacMillan, *Greek Island Embroideries* (Boston: Museum of Fine Arts, n.d.), n.p.

39. See Roderick Taylor, *Embroidery of the Greek Islands* (Brooklyn, NY: Interlink Books, 1998), 68–69.

40. Ibid., 64.

41. Information from the record books in the Textile Department of the Victoria and Albert Museum. I thank Linda Parry and Linda Wooley for facilitating my research concerning these embroideries.

42. U. T. Sirelius, *The Ryijy-Rugs of Finland: A Historical Study* (Helsinki: Otava, 1926), 6–7.

43. Ibid., plates 6-20.

44. Ibid., 175–176. *Ryijy* with straight stripes related to those of figure 57 are typical of the Gustavian period. The running border of the MOIFA example is related to that of a *ryijy* dated 1807, illustrated in Sirelius, *Ryijy-Rugs*, plate 58, n.p. Because the drawing of the tulips in a vase in the MOIFA bedcover is a freer, less detailed version than that depicted in the book, it is possible that the MOIFA bedcover dates slightly later, though it might simply be by another hand. Pirkko Sihko, curator, National Museum of Finland, who over sees a collection including more than six hundred *ryijy*, has confirmed the date of approximately 1800 for figure 57.

45. Sirelius, *Ryijy-Rugs*, 1.

46. Ibid., 29.

47. The first modern *ryijy* was exhibited at the 1900 Paris World Exposition. Designed by Akseli Gallen-Kallela, it was described as "one independent of folk design and folk use of color." See Leena Svinhufvud, "Finnish Textiles en Route to Modernity," in Marianne Aav and Nina Stritzler-Levine, eds., *Finnish Modern Design: Utopian Ideals and Everyday Realities, 1930–1997* (New Haven, CT: Yale University Press, 1998), 194.

48. Ibid., 193.

3. Sleeping in the Closet

"In a cosy bed much mischief can occur."
— *Welsh song*

Annie Carlano

Sleeping in the Closet

Figure 59
Cupboard bed, Älvros,
Harjedalen, Sweden, early
nineteenth century.
Painted and carved wood in
folk baroque style of rural
Sweden.

Figure 60
Double-decker cupboard
beds, Mora Parish, Dalarna,
Stockholm, Sweden,
early nineteenth century.
Unpainted wood.

When my friends Valerie and John needed to find space in their five-hundred-square-foot New York apartment for their young son Steve's bedroom, they rejected the usual solution—creating a mezzanine loft space—because they wanted to preserve their high ceilings. Instead, they put Steve's bed in the closet. With this choice they unknowingly adopted one of the most fascinating yet quintessentially practical (at least by the standards of its time) furniture designs ever created: the European "bed incognito," disguised as part of a wall or masquerading as another type of furniture. Called built-ins, cupboard beds, and box beds, these forms took the idea of the canopy bed and the alcove bed one step further by creating an enclosed sleeping chamber that was an integral part of the interior architectural wall plan. Built-ins were conceived of and constructed as part of the house itself, rather than as furniture. Box beds and cupboard beds, terms used interchangeably, were semi-detached or freestanding structures that were placed against a wall in such a way that they blended with the interior wainscoting or with the facades of armoires and other furniture.

Beds built into the corners of rooms, from the wall surfaces, date to the Viking era.[1] Not surprisingly, this approach to bed design developed in a part of the world where keeping warm while sleeping was a big challenge, exacerbated by the fact that early Viking houses consisted of only one room for the entire family. Norse people faced the same conundrum as modern-day New Yorkers: where to put beds in such small spaces. Throughout Scandinavia these early one-room rural homes had low ceilings, so the most efficient use of space was to put the bed in a corner *(fig. 59)*. Multiple beds might be organized along a side wall, *en enfilade,* or sometimes, among large families, double-decker style. Such traditions continued into the nineteenth century *(fig. 60)*.

Demonstrating a Scandinavian penchant for aesthetically pleasing interiors, the earliest extant built-ins were either lavishly painted or skillfully carved and were adorned with many patterned textiles as pillows, bed curtains, and coverlets. In Norway they were covered with floral painting *(rosmaling)*; in Denmark, masterful cabinetry featured fine woods, simply but exquisitely worked; and in Sweden, accomplished craftsmanship is evident in both the woodworking and the weavings and embroideries of the bed.[2] The Swedish built-in bed was practically wallpapered with textiles suspended from the bed ceiling and covering the interior walls. In this way it mimicked the interior decoration of the room itself, which was swathed in fabric from floor to ceiling, resembling the inside of a tent *(fig. 61)*. Identifying with this tradition, the Swedish artist Carl Larsson created a bed for "Papa's bedroom" in his own house in 1899 that to him symbolized the inherent modernity of Swedish rural design *(fig. 62)*.

Built-in beds were ubiquitous in the Netherlands, from city to country, from the houses of the Dutch bourgeoisie to the home of the baker. In a small country with a large population and a miserable climate, the popularity of built-in beds is easy to comprehend. Since at least 1750, fishermen's cottages on the island of Marken in the Zuyder Zee (now the Ijsselmeer) and in most of the northeastern part of the country were constructed with beds built into the walls, in interiors that had as their chief distinguishing feature a *horror vacui* composition of decorative ceramic plates and other bric-a-brac *(fig. 63)*. These cupboard beds were not just sleeping places. Closed up during the day with fancy Dutch printed textiles, they functioned as display shelves for other prized textiles and sentimental objects, many of which were souvenirs from whaling journeys to Scandinavia, Scotland, and England.[3]

Classic Dutch box beds were conceived as part of a room's elaborate wall paneling. In the seventeenth-century middle-class interior shown in figure 64, we see a typical room with a built-in bed. Rather than being part of a flat expanse of wall into which a niche was constructed and then concealed by curtains or doors, this built-in projects out from the wall, looking very much like the architectonic Renaissance beds from which this type seems to have emerged. Strategically placed in a corner, adjacent to the hearth, the bed stayed relatively warm. Dutch built-in beds characteristically displayed bed curtains and a valance, designed en suite with the valance of the hearth and other furnishing textiles of the interior, from table rugs to window curtains.

Arriving in what was to them the New World, the Dutch introduced their vernacular architecture and domestic habits. The Jan Martense Schneck family, middle-class Dutch Americans, built their house in 1675 in Mill Island, now part of Long Island, New York. It was eventually acquired by the Brooklyn Museum, whose curators established that cupboard beds had made up part of the interior. No physical evidence of cupboard beds existed in this house or others in the area, but research into inventories and oral histories showed that seventeenth-century Dutch Americans commissioned cupboard

Figure 61
Carl Larsson,
Namnsdag på härbret, c. 1899.
Watercolor and ink on paper.
Nationalmuseum, Stockholm,
Sweden.

Figure 62
Carl Larsson,
Pappas rum, c. 1899.
Watercolor and ink on paper.
Nationalmuseum, Stockholm,
Sweden.

Figure 63
Built-in bed, Marken,
Netherlands, c. 1750,
at the Netherlands
Open Air Museum
(Openluchtmuseum).

beds from carpenters for homes and taverns. One such document reads, "In the recess [build] two bedsteads, one in the front room and one in the inside room, with a pantry at the end of the bedstead," indicating the cupboardlike nature of the built-in. These cupboard beds would have been placed near the hearth and decorated with the coordinating room fabric, in the Dutch manner. An inventory from 1689 describes a set as "1 suite sage curtains and vallons with silk fringe."[4]

Despite political and demographic changes over the centuries, in at least one household the cupboard bed seems to have been in use in Brooklyn until the late nineteenth century. According to an elderly woman in 1964, her mother had told her that she remembered a cupboard bed in the home of Nicolas Schneck—a descendant of J. M. Schneck—at that time.[5]

Nowhere was the tradition of the built-in bed and the cupboard bed richer and more varied, more pervasive, or more culturally significant than in the region of Brittany, France. A craggy peninsula that juts into the Atlantic,

Figure 64
An oak bed built in as part of the wall paneling, Dordrecht, Netherlands, 1626.
Rijksmuseum, Amsterdam.

Figure 65
Postcard depicting a *lit clos*, or cupboard bed, Brittany, France, c. 1900. Its caption reads: "2103. Bretagne. Le Coucher de la Mariée; Très émue, la jeune épousée n'ose: se dévêtir devant son mari [The bride's wedding night: filled with emotion, the young bride doesn't dare undress herself in front of her husband]." Private collection.

Brittany is the westernmost part of France. In two of its four *départements,* those of Finistère and Morbihan, one finds the majority of the cupboard beds. They are called *gwele kloz* in Bretagne and *lit clos* in French, both meaning "closed bed." Why cupboard beds developed in this part of France remains a mystery, considering that the climate, although damp, is quite mild. Some researchers speculate that early settlers from the north initiated the form here. Reflecting this heritage, the earliest *lits clos* display abstract geometric and botanical symbols that have been linked to the Celtic culture of mid-sixth-century Brittany and to Irish art of the high Middle Ages *(fig. 65).*[6]

Dating to the first half of the seventeenth century in Léon, Finistère, the *lit carrosse,* a cupboard bed on wheels, and the *lit d'angle,* a cupboard bed built into a corner, emerged as the first types of *lits clos* in Brittany. These earliest beds, made of thick, blocky oak or chestnut, were rendered more delicate in appearance by means of an accomplished repertoire of carved, turned, and pierced decoration that often filled two or three sides of the bed surface from foot to pediment. Rosette motifs, branches and leaves, spirals, diamonds, and intricate ornamental friezes cleverly concealed the door or opening at the center.

Framed by balustrades, the single door opening was typical of beds from Léon. The *lits clos* of most other regions were closed by means of a sliding door. Opened at night to allow air to circulate while people slept, the door left the mattresses, bed linens, bedcovers, and occupants of the bed all visible. With the door closed during the day, the bed looked much like a storage cupboard. As the principal piece of furniture of the farmhouse, it functioned additionally as a sideboard and mantle, the place where families displayed treasures such as fine laces, faience religious figures, rosaries, holy water fonts, and, in later periods, beloved photographs. Frightening as it might seem today, the *lit clos* often had sconces attached to hold candles.

Figure 66
Henry Mosler (1841–1920),
Return of the Prodigal, c.1883.
Oil on canvas.
Departmental Museum of Brittany,
inv. D.80.1.1. (Dépôt de l'Etat).

How did one enter the *lit clos?* Many such beds were designed with an attached or detachable combination of bench and low chest *(fig. 66)*. One stepped onto this piece of furniture and then climbed into the inner chamber of the bed. One could sit on it while visiting with those in bed or while putting on one's stockings and shoes in the morning. It also served as a table for food and drink. As a chest, it was the place where the bedclothes and other items were stored. In Léon and Cornouaille, this type of *lit clos* was placed in the compact common room, sometimes the only room of the house, across from the dining table, so that the bench also served as seating furniture for the family at mealtime.[7] Ingeniously designed, such rooms enabled residents to use every square meter of space efficiently and in an aesthetically pleasing manner.

Sleeping in a *lit clos,* raised high off the ground, protected people from being annoyed or threatened by ever-present domestic animals, livestock, and predators. According to "la legende du lit clos," these beds were originally invented to safeguard sleepers against hungry wolves, akin to the one in the tale of Little Red Riding Hood. Wolves were believed to enter the house and eat infants in their cribs. Pigs, too, were thought to enter houses and munch on sleeping babies' noses and ears. Ubiquitous chickens pecked the faces of the wee ones. For these reasons, it was said, farmers decided to put their young children on shelves in cupboards, to sleep undisturbed during the day while the elders tended to their work in the fields.[8]

Eventually the whole family slept in cupboard beds, but around 1800, in the countryside near Quimper, Finistère, only the "masters" of the house enjoyed this questionable privilege. Other family members and servants slept nearby in the common room on blankets, where they may actually have been more comfortable. By most accounts, sleeping in a traditional *lit clos* was awkward and unhealthy. Measuring about just over 8 feet high by 4 ½ to 6 feet long (2.5 by 1.4–1.8 m), the average *lit clos,* like the Scandinavian built-in, permitted one to sleep only in a half-seated position. To stay warm, the occupants had to keep the doors completely shut, and a well-crafted bed was nearly airtight, reflecting prevailing medical ideas about sleeping with windows closed to protect people from the damp night air. Add bed linens that were infrequently changed, people who seldom bathed, and communal foods left out on the bench, and the *lit clos* became a breeding ground for infectious diseases. People who took to the *lit clos* as their sick bed often became even sicker.[9] Hardly the romantic, cozy nest that inspired the nostalgic yet edgy contemporary designs of the Bouroullec brothers (see chapter 6), the traditional *lit clos* had a serious flaw in that its form did not follow its function of providing a good night's sleep.

Perhaps the artisans of Morbihan, the *département* to the southeast of Finistère, had this flaw in mind when they developed the *lit demi-clos,* also known as the *lit mi-clos.* This style of cupboard bed was doorless; a large opening in the center of the façade permitted easy entrance and exit and the circulation of air. Yet it seems that sleeping in a *lit demi-clos* was no more comfortable than sleeping in its neighboring *lit clos.* In 1794–1795 Jacques Cambry traveled in the region and commented that "the height of these sleeping floor planks is sometimes only about two feet; [in the *lit demi-clos*] they sleep on a bale of oats or rye, without a mattress, without feather beds or sheets, many covered only with a kind of hay sack, few with wool blankets."[10] Sometimes curtains and even a valance covered the opening, providing greater warmth and a more decorative surface.

Today, in homes in Morbihan and Finistère, it is rare to find a complete *lit clos* or *lit mi-clos.* What one does find, not only in Brittany but in the homes of Bretons living in Paris and of others who collect or simply enjoy living with traditional French art, is the flea-market-purchased façade of the *lit clos* or *mi-clos,* detached from its "cupboard" and installed in a foyer or living room. It is charged with a sense of *temps perdu* and, at the same time, of Breton "shabby chic" *(fig. 67).*

This nostalgic decorative use would probably have come as no surprise to the great French ethnographer Georges-Henri Rivière, who traveled the most remote parts of France in the mid-twentieth century, collecting objects for the Musée National des Arts et des Traditions Populaires in Paris (which he had established in 1937) that were in danger of disappearing from French cultural life. Going from village to village in Brittany, he amassed forty-five notebooks of his observations from 1941 to 1945.[11] Even at that time he noted the way farmers were beginning to sell their traditional *lits clos* to antiques dealers and replace them with simple post beds, to make their homes more fashionable.

Four other distinct kinds of *lits clos* deserve mention. The first—the most eccentric and fewest in number—was the double-decker type with four doors, known as a coach bed, possibly because it was inspired by berths in a ship's cabin. Most double-decker *lits clos* come from the outlying areas of Rennes (Ille-et-Vilaine). Second, many beds from what is affectionately called the "pays Bigouden," the countryside around Pont-l'Abbé, known for its inhabitants' eccentric dress, feature decorations made with large-headed copper nails. Motifs similar to those carved on other beds, as well as mottoes, names, initials, and dates, are hammered into the wood—an inexpensive way of creating patterns. Third, although I have never read about or seen one, there are said to exist, in situ, *lits clos* designed especially to fit the curvilinear interiors of Brittany's lighthouses.[12] And fourth, on the island of Ousseant, off the coast of Brest (Finistère),

Figure 67
Façade and bench of a *lit clos* used as a decorative furnishing. Finistère, Brittany, France, 2005. Chestnut, 68¾ x 73¾ x 19¼ in. (175 x 187.5 x 49 cm). Collection Fruman, France.

the *lits clos* are painted, usually blue and white in honor of the Virgin Mary.

Built-in and cupboard beds found popularity in several other regions of France as well, predominantly the Auvergne, the Pyrenees, the Dauphiné (which includes the Alps), and Alsace. In Haute-Auvergne, cupboard beds and built-in beds were in use from at least 1759. An inventory from that year described three beds in the common room of the laborer Jean Siscans as "appuyés au mur" (against the wall) and another bed in the adjoining room as "adherant au mur" (adhering to the wall). The home of the merchant Guillaume Loussert, one of the wealthier people in Haute-Auvergne at the time, had nine beds in the main part of the house and four *mi-clos* in the cellar where the servants slept.[13] Cabinetmaking in the Auvergne differed from that of Brittany in the simplicity of its surface designs. The woodworking of the beds had one motif—for example, a heart or a scallop—at the top center of the façade, with architectural incised sections. Adapted from mainstream prototypes, these bed designs nonetheless expressed regional aesthetics.

In the Auvergne, as well as in the Pyrenees, the *lit abri* was used by shepherds keeping watch over their flocks. This ingenious *lit clos,* perhaps the first *wagon lit,* allowed shepherds to be near their animals throughout the night.

Do people anywhere in the world continue to sleep in traditional built-in, box, or cupboard beds? Writing in 1952, Reginald Reynolds noted that in Scottish Caledonia people still slept in box beds.[14] More than fifty years later, I suspect that the custom of sleeping in the closet is more a phenomenon of urban Western life than anything else. My friends' son Steve has grown up and out of the closet, and his parents have moved to a large loft—but those tiny New York studio apartments and their counterparts throughout the urban world can be seen as the cupboard beds of our time.

Notes

1. Janet S. Stewart, *The Folk Arts of Norway* (New York: Dover, 1972), 44.

2. For depictions of firmly documented Danish built-in beds, see Axel Steensberg, *Danske bondemøbler* (Copenhagen: Alfr. G. Hassings, 1949), figs. 172–202.

3. *Guide: National Folk Museum, the Netherlands Open-Air Museum* (Arnhem, 1985), 83–84.

4. Kevin L. Stanton, *Dutch by Design: Tradition and Change in Two Brooklyn Houses. The Schneck Houses at the Brooklyn Museum* (New York: Brooklyn Museum in association with Phaidon Universe, 1990), 34–36.

5. Ibid., 36.

6. This view is still widely held, although some scholars find it problematic. See, for example, Jean Cuisenier, *French Folk Art* (Tokyo: Kodansha, 1976), 106.

7. Philippe Le Stum, *Arts Populaires de Bretagne* (n.p.: Éditions Ouest-France, 1995), 56. A room with this type of *lit clos* from a house in Goulieu, Finistère, was installed in the main gallery of the Musée National des Arts et des Traditions Populaires, Paris. This museum is to move to Marseilles in 2006, under the new name Musée National des Arts et des Traditions de France et de la Méditerranée.

8. This story, well known to most Bretons, is recounted on a postcard, dated about 1900, in the collection of the Musée National des Arts et des Traditions Populaires. It was around that time that an effort was made to market the costumes, regional foods, and unusual traditions of Brittany, including that of the *lit clos,* through postcards depicting "authentic" cultural *moeurs.* Most of these images were studio shots using actual historic objects.

9. Information from L. Mareschal, *La galerie des moeurs, usages et coutumes des Bretons de l'Armorique* (Paris: n.p., 1808), as quoted in Le Stum, *Arts Populaires de Bretagne,* 55.

10. Jacques Cambry, *Voyage en Finistère* (1798), cited in Le Stum, *Arts Populaires de Bretagne,* 58.

11. Even during World War II, Brittany was an isolated and relatively safe place.

12. Information from a conversation with Marie-Claude and Michel Joblin-Depalle, specialists in French regional art who have lived and traveled extensively in Brittany, May 2004.

13. Jean-Claude Roc, *Meubles populaires de Haute-Auvergne* (Brioude en Auvergne: Editions Watel, 1995), 88.

14. Reginald Reynolds, *Beds, with Many Noteworthy Instances of Lying On, Under or About Them* (New York: Andre Deutsch, 1952), 84.

"Sleep lingers all our lifetime about our eyes, as night hovers all day in the boughs of the fir tree." — *Ralph Waldo Emerson*

Bobbie Sumberg

Sleeping on the Move

Figure 68
Pavel Kuznetsov
(1878–1968),
Girl Sleeping under a Tent.
Tretyakov Gallery, Moscow, Russia.

Figure 69
The black goat-hair tent of
Ramazan and Aisha pitched
in the mountains near
Karaman, Turkey,
June 2004.

Nomads, people who travel from place to place taking their dwellings and worldly possessions with them, have existed since the first humans left their place of genesis on foot. Known as travelers, gypsies, hippies, and RVers, they still exist today. Nomadic pastoralists—people who move with their domesticated flocks to seasonal pastures and live in portable dwellings—got a comparatively late start in human history. It all began about 800 BCE with the tent-dwelling Scythians, the first people to follow their livestock out of Central Asia, mounted on horses and sometimes camels. Since then, nomadic pastoralists have inhabited Mongolia, Tibet, Central Asia, Iran, Turkey, North, East, and West Africa, and the Arabian peninsula.

Settled society has contradictory feelings about nomads. On one hand, they are perceived as troublemakers—as thieves, as environment-destroying keepers of goats and sheep, as people who are politically unpredictable and violence prone. On the other, they are seen as the pure embodiment of living close to nature—as romantic dwellers close to the Garden of Eden *(fig. 68)*. They are both feared and envied and thus provide material for the artistic imagination.

Nomads need shelter that is portable, weatherproof, and easily constructed of available materials. A nomadic dwelling has to be flexible enough to function under varied conditions and constraints. Remarkably, among all the different peoples who travel with animals in all the diverse landscapes of the world, two forms of shelter predominate. The tent that is widely used in Tibet, Southwest Asia, Africa, the Middle East, and parts of Turkey is essentially formless. A large piece of woven wool cloth or leather, or a set of reed or grass mats, is given shape by a rudimentary frame made of individual poles or sticks, or else it is draped over poles and tensioned with ropes. The shape can be changed to meet environmental conditions or the owner's aesthetic. The tent can nestle into the protection of surrounding trees or it can stand free, like a house *(fig. 69)*. Rectangular tents are the most common, except in Africa, where circular, oval, or dome-topped rectangular tents are more prevalent.[1]

Figure 70
Storage bags and bedding in the tent, June 2004.

The other common form of portable housing still in use is the yurt. Called *ger* in Mongolia, *boz uy* in Kyrgyzstan, and *öy* among the Turkmen, the yurt consists of a circular wooden lattice framework covered with wool felt. A domed crown with a hole or skylight completes the structure. The frame folds up into sections that pack easily onto a camel. Yurts are so comfortable and so ingrained in Central Asian life that the Mongolian city of Ulaanbaatar is surrounded by suburbs made up entirely of stationary yurts.[2]

In a dwelling without interior walls or rooms, the division of space into public and private, eating and sleeping, or male and female areas takes on a symbolic dimension. Food storage and cooking—associated with women—occupy one side of the tent or yurt, while entertaining guests and eating—associated with men—take place on the other side of an invisible line. Different groups draw the line differently, but the basic concept is the same. A nomad entering another nomad's dwelling would know where he or she should sit according to this division of space.

Among the Yörük of southeastern Turkey, the tent is set up on the ground; the floor consists of woven textiles and felts laid on the dirt. Of course shoes are removed when one enters a tent, to minimize the tracking of dirt and animal manure into the living space. Arranged against the back wall of the tent are the handwoven storage bags that hold clothes and nonperishable foods. Bedding is folded and piled up next to the bags, so that it can be easily spread out for the night *(fig. 70)*.

For the majority of tent dwellers, bed means textiles, not furniture. In the tent of Ramazan and Aisha in the mountains of southeastern Turkey, the ground, covered with cloths and pads that provide a minimum of cushioning, is the sleeping surface. Pads might be handmade using store-bought fabrics stuffed with fiber from the herds. Families who still travel with camels, as Ramazan and Aisha do, stuff sleeping pads, pillows, and quilts with camel wool to keep warm. Families who raise sheep use wool to make the bedding. Black goat hair from the animals that many nomads keep for their milk is used to weave the tent fabric and the hard-wearing cloths that go directly on the ground. Sometimes plastic mats replace these goat-hair *çul*.

Laid on top of the cloths, felted sheep's-wool mats, formerly made by the nomads themselves, are now made in workshops in Konya and Afyon. Felt mats are common floor coverings among nomads all over Anatolia and Central Asia, but wealthy

Figure 71
Sleeping in the tent,
June 2004.

Figure 72
In the village of Kiseçik, Mrs. Yarimali stands in front of her bedding, which is stored in an alcove built into the wall of the house, June 2004.

nomads might have carpets woven by the women and girls of the family to sit and sleep on. Coverlets stuffed with wool keep the sleepers warm, a custom borrowed from Turkish villagers beginning in the early 1970s. Before that nomads used woven camel-hair blankets in natural tan or brown with simple stripe patterns made from white and colored sheep's wool. Used until they wore out, such blankets are scarce now.

Household activities take place inside the tent. Over a small fire in a hearth near the entrance, family members brew tea, cook food, and bake flatbread on a metal pan. They eat their meals in the tent; children play there and then nap where they fall *(fig. 71)*. The whole tent is a bedroom, and the floor and its coverings, a bed.

Some provisions are made for the privacy of newlyweds and sometimes for the head of the family, depending on the group. In these cases, residents hang a curtain along a line inside the tent or yurt, keeping it raised during the day and letting it down at night to provide a semblance of seclusion from the rest of the family. After the birth of

Figure 73
Sleeping rug *tülü*
c. 1940
Goat hair, cotton
75 x 50in. (190.5 x 127cm)
Museum of International Folk Art,
gift of Mr. & Mrs. Gordon Campbell.

the first baby, this privilege is revoked, and the young couple joins the rest of the family in sleeping either lined up in a row or scattered across the floor.

Although nomadic pastoralists in Central Asia, Iran, and surrounding areas are great weavers, not all nomads weave. Neither the Rendille nomads of northern Kenya nor Somali nomads weave textiles from animal fibers, although they keep camels, sheep, and goats. They do make mats from reeds and grasses for sitting and sleeping. Somali women weave a box from palm fronds to hold their bedding. This *abaxad* is then covered with leather and decorated with cowry shells and beads.

Neither do all pastoral nomads eschew a bed raised off the floor. William of Rubruck, a Franciscan friar who began a three-year journey to Mongolia in 1253 in the hope of promoting Christianity among the Mongol nomads, left the earliest Western account of their life and material culture. He mentioned beds, couches, and coffers that held bedding, which were transported on carts and brought into the yurt each time camp was moved. One wonders what the furniture looked like, but William did not describe it except to say that it was gilded.[3] The Khazaks, in the area around Lake Balkhash and the Aral Sea, have also used wooden beds inside their yurts since the nineteenth century. Judging from photographs, these beds appear to have concave headboards and footboards and to be piled with pillows and quilts.[4] They do not come apart for easy transport but instead must be carried from camp to camp on a cart. The use of wagons and carts by the nomadic Mongols was widespread until the Middle Ages, allowing for the transport of heavy, bulky, and fragile items such as beds and porcelain teacups acquired from the Chinese.

Some African nomads—from Mauritania in the west to Kenya in the east—on the other hand, use beds that come apart for travel. In some tents the beds are free-standing; in others the bedstead is integrated into the tent frame, increasing the stability of the structure. Fellata-Baggare women in Chad and Sudan use the poles that make the bed frame to form part of the camel saddle used to transport the tent and its furnishings to the next grazing ground.[5] A bed off the ground provides some protection from the poisonous insects and snakes that inhabit the desert, but one would think it would be awfully bulky to transport over the distances that people travel. As Labelle Prussin made clear in her book *African Nomadic Architecture,* the tent, together with the bed and the rest of the furnishings, is not simply a shelter from the harshness of the desert but is intricately entwined with African nomads' conceptions of marriage, family, community, creativity, and appropriate gender behavior.

Although fast disappearing as a viable lifestyle, nomadic pastoralism still exists in many places. As nomads settle down in villages and houses, they retain some of their nomadic ways in their everyday lives. In Anatolian villages, houses are often quite simple, with a minimum of furniture. People keep piles of bedding in cupboards, folded and ready to take down at night *(fig. 72)*. No rooms are designated specifically for sleeping. Family members lay rugs, mats, and deep-pile textiles called *tülü* on the floor wherever the urge for sleep strikes *(fig. 73)*. When the house replaces the tent in Africa, the bed retains its symbolic meaning and physical placement in the home, even if the materials and the surroundings are different. The nomadic sense and aesthetic remain.

Nomads do not always follow goats and sheep to grazing; some follow their whims. Itinerant peddlers, traders, salespeople, and laborers travel seasonally or inces-santly to earn a living, but they do not generally carry their homes and all their worldly possessions with them. Instead, the nomadic, traveling life is associated with the Romany-speaking people. Often mistrusted and misunderstood, the Roma, also known

Figure 75
The interior of Gypsy Queen
Phoebe Stanley's *vardo*,
showing the bed.
Long Island Museum of American
Art, History, and Carriages.

as Gypsies, were forced from their settled life in northern India by invasions in the eleventh century. Moving in a generally northwesterly direction, they passed through Central Asia into central Europe and eventually, by the early sixteenth century, were spread across the continent and Great Britain. Originally traveling on foot and with pack animals, they began to use the wagon, or *vardo,* by the mid-nineteenth century *(fig. 74).*

In Great Britain, five types of wagons were available to the Roma. Distinguished by the shape of the body and the place in which they were built, they all shared common features: they were built by non-Roma, or Gadjo; Romany women owned them and their furnishings; and the interiors included storage space, seating, a stove for cooking and warmth, and a loftlike bed at the front of the wagon protected by a curtain *(fig. 75).* Some caravans were highly decorated and hung with elaborate curtains and textiles, whereas others were plain. A wagon was the Roma woman's most prized possession and status symbol.

Although few Roma today use a *vardo* in their daily lives, such vehicles do exist and are even built by a few wagon makers in England. But most Gypsies have replaced

Figure 74
Wagon *(vardo)* that belo[ng]
to Gypsy Queen Phoebe
Stanley of West Natick,
Massachusetts, c. 1880.
Long Island Museum of Ame[rican]
Art, History, and Carriages,

wagons with trucks and travel trailers, or caravans, perhaps more practical modes of transportation but definitely lacking the aesthetics and character of the *vardo*. The *vardo* appears to have been the inspiration for the sheep wagon, first built in Rawlins, Wyoming, in 1884 by James Candlish, son of Scottish immigrants. Used by sheep-herders as transportation and shelter while in the high summer pastures of the American West, sheep wagons had dimensions and interior layouts uncannily similar to those of the *vardo*.

The *vardo* also seems a likely prototype for the modern travel trailer. Long before self-contained recreational vehicles came on the scene, compact living units were pulled by cars and trucks, enabling people to travel independently of hotels and public transportation. Many people who long to leave behind the sedentary life of house and city to hit the road as a nomad cherish this kind of freedom and mobility.

In the United States, converted school buses and delivery vans became popular alternatives to the Airstream and the Winnebago in the 1960s and 1970s. Structures built onto the bed of a pickup truck allowed the creativity and personal style of the maker to shine *(fig. 76)*. Whether a mobile mattress or a compact living space, the sleeping area often combined the coziness of a ship's cabin or wagon with the funk of the hippie era. The barter fair—a gathering place for back-to-the-landers and alternative travelers and traders—is a great venue for homemade mobile homes.

For sedentary people, tent dwelling has always been a romantic notion. For explorers, travelers, and military personnel, sleeping in tents has often been the only option at hand. Sleeping in a tent did not always mean sleeping on the ground. Folding beds called camp beds have been in use since the eighteenth century, although the earliest folding beds, found in the tomb of King Tutankhamen, were made from wood in the fourteenth century BCE *(fig. 77)*. Folding wooden beds also found popularity among European royalty in the fifteenth and sixteenth centuries, as did vacationing in a tent camp in the forest.[6] These beds were not strictly practical, because they had canopies and curtains and were highly decorated, but they were portable with the help of a retinue of servants.

One of the most famous sleepers on a camp bed, or *lit de campagne,* was Napoleon, emperor of France. Both he and his vanquisher, the Duke of Wellington, slept on camp beds even when not on campaign. Napoleon is said to have died on his folding iron bed in captivity on the island of St. Helena in the South Atlantic.

Victorian travelers such as Gertrude Bell, who wandered the Middle East and Iraq in the years before World War I, traveled in style with hired men leading pack animals carrying everything from tents, china dinnerware, and writing desks to camp beds and bedding. Others, male and female, traveled rough, needing only blankets to wrap around themselves when night fell.

Travelers sleeping in an inn or hostel often carried their blankets with them, as do today's youth hostelers. Medieval pilgrims visiting shrines and sacred sites all over Europe were accommodated in monasteries and inns. They wore blue woolen cloaks large enough to wrap around themselves when they got into bed at night. Coat by day and blanket by night, this garment distinguished people on pilgrimage from common travelers.

The bedroll developed from the dual-purpose outer garment for travelers who carried their belongings themselves, not using porters or pack animals. Originally just a few blankets tied together with a string, it grew into a sleeping system that was compact and easily portable. Cowboys in the American West wrapped their blankets in a piece of heavy canvas that, when laid out on the ground and folded up around the sleeper, became a relatively weatherproof sack, a personal shelter that could be tied onto the back of the saddle. Bedrolls are available for purchase still and are used by reenactors and aspiring cowboys.

Inuit and other Arctic peoples since time unknown have used sleeping bags to weather the extreme temperatures of winter. Caribou skins sewn together with the hair side in, laid on a mattress of caribou skin with the hair side down, on a bed platform of packed snow, provide the warmth and comfort needed for a good night's sleep. Arctic explorers quickly learned that local materials and styles were essential to their survival and adopted the parkas, footwear, and sleeping bags of the natives *(fig. 78)*.

A byway in the development of tents and portable sleeping accommodations was the product known as the valise or sleeping valise. These heavy, waterproof canvas shelters with felt mattress were semi-rigid, folded up into a suitcase, and folded out into a sack that completely enclosed the sleeper. Advertised as insect-proof and completely impermeable, these kits were sold to British colonial officers on their way to India and Africa.[7] Imagine how uncomfortable it must have been to spend a tropical African night buckled securely into an unventilated canvas bag—not just a shelter but a portable sauna, too.

Lack of specialized equipment did not stop mountain men and naturalists from exploring the high mountains of the American Rockies and Sierra Nevada. John Muir, founder of the Sierra Club and champion of wilderness in California, spent the summer of 1869 herding sheep in the mountains above Yosemite Valley, carrying only blankets for bedding.[8] Modern-day sleeping bags were first manufactured in Canada in 1885 by the Woods Company and in Norway by Ajungilak to serve the Arctic explorers of the time.[9] Originally made from kapok and canvas, these heavy, not very portable bags improved with the use of down and the development of synthetic fabrics and fillings. Now, hikers

Figure 76
Boston, Massachusetts, 1976. Patty Smith and Jack Sumberg gaze from the bedside window of *Decentralize Everything* before heading west.

and campers have a wealth of options, from a simple insulating pad that offers no cushioning of the hard ground to a lightweight inflatable mattress and a full-fledged camp bed or cot in a two-room tent. Sleeping bags of down or synthetics, roomy or spare, covered with slippery nylon or cozy cotton, cater to anyone's desire to indulge in the illusion of the nomadic past, in a tent and on the move.

Notes

1. Labelle Prussin, *African Nomadic Architecture: Space, Place, and Gender* (Washington, DC: Smithsonian Institution Press, 1995).

2. David Pearson, *Circle Houses: Yurts, Tipis, and Benders* (White River Junction, VT: Chelsea Green, 2001), 10.

3. The *Journey of William of Rubruck to the Eastern Parts of the World, 1253–55, as Narrated by Himself, with Two Accounts of the Earlier Journey of John of Pian de Carpine,* trans. and ed. William Woodville Rockhill (London: Hakluyt Society, 1900).

4. See Vladimir N. Basilov, ed., *Nomads of Eurasia* (Los Angeles: Natural History Museum of Los Angeles County, 1989), 131, for a 1908 photograph inside a Khazak yurt.

5. Prussin, *African Nomadic Architecture,* 56.

6. Lawrence Wright, *Warm and Snug: The History of the Bed* (London: Routledge and Keegan Paul, 1962), 61.

7. *Yesterday's Shopping: The Army and Navy Stores Catalogue 1907* (Devon, England: David and Charles Reprints, 1980).

8. John Muir, *My First Summer in the Sierra* (Boston: Houghton Mifflin, 1911).

9. A press release history of the Ajungilak Company cites Francis Fox Tucker as the inventor of the modern sleeping bag, in 1863. From the description, the bag sounds like the cowboy bedroll with a buttoned opening and an attached ground cloth.

Figure 77
Folding bed from the tomb of
Tutankhamun. Egyptian-
Dynasty XVIII.
Thebes: Valley of the Kings.
Metropolitan Museum of Art.

Figure 78
Sleeping bag used during
a camping trip in October
1888, formerly on the Greeley
expedition.
Library of Congress. LC-USZ62-
25362.

5. Sleeping on the Road

"No one realizes how beautiful it is to travel until he comes home and rests his head on his old, familiar pillow." — *Lin Yutang*

Bobbie Sumberg

Sleeping on the Road

Figure 79
Emigrants in steerage aboard the *Samuel Hop*, 1849. Woodblock print.

Figure 80
Interior view of Norfolk and Washington Steamboat Company cabin, c. 1900. Francis Benjamin Johnston Collection, Library of Congress, LC-USZ62-99488.

A comfortable bed and a good night's sleep while on the road epitomize the luxury of travel—the luxury of taking time to get to one's destination, the luxury of the past, when everything seems to have been more stylish, and the luxury of going first class. Nothing is more romantic than the idea of slipping into a berth in a sleeper car on the Orient Express as it clacks through cities and the wild unknown expanses of central Europe on its way to Istanbul. The reality of the experience seems quite different when you discover that you can reach out and touch the other wall of the cabin from your narrow berth. A claustrophobe fares poorly in a train berth. With the relentless speeding up of leisure travel in the twentieth century, sleeping comfortably while crossing a continent or an ocean has become a luxury nearly unattainable.

Historically, people traveled more out of necessity than out of desire. Transportation by foot, on pack or riding animal, or by human-powered boat meant that journeys were long and uncomfortable. For the wealthy, staying in an inn was possible but not exactly comfortable. The poor generally stayed home, equally uncomfortably.

As European knowledge of navigation and improved sailing technology developed, long-distance travel by sea became more available. The so-called age of exploration—the fourteenth to the seventeenth century—also begat the age of travel writing.[1]

The only way to get across the Atlantic Ocean before 1840, whether a person traveled for business, government, military, or survival reasons, was on a sailing ship. The journey was long—up to two months—and made dangerous by the presence of icebergs, deadly storms and fogs, and the kind of crushing tedium that led to mutiny. Ships were not fitted out to be comfortable, and sleeping accommodations were the most basic that could be considered decent for paying customers. The sailing packets of 1820–1840, American ships that carried goods and passengers and left on a regular schedule, were faster than previous ships and therefore an improvement. Although designed for passengers as well as cargo, the packets did not offer their cabin passengers luxurious or even comfortable sleeping quarters. The mattress on the narrow berth was no more than planks covered with sacking. The actress and passenger Fanny Kemble moaned, "Oh, for a bed! A real bed! Any manner of bed, but a bed on shipboard!"[2] Steerage offered only a rough berth between decks and a place on deck to cook meals. It was often the only choice available to immigrants seeking a new life in the United States (fig. 79).

During the packet era, mechanics and inventors worked furiously to harness the power of steam. Despite many false starts and unexplored byways, steam engines of all sorts emerged, powering textile mills, locomotives, and many kinds of marine transportation. The first steamships, deep-draft boats that also carried sails, ran up and down the rivers and coasts of Great Britain and North America, transporting goods and people. The first transatlantic voyages in which steam engines provided the main source of locomotion took place in 1839.[3] Two rival steamships, the *Great Western* and the *British Queen,* chugged across the treacherous North Atlantic in fifteen or sixteen days, vying for the title not only of the fastest boat but also the most luxurious. Passenger appointments were taken seriously now, because these vessels carried not heavy cargo but mail and passengers. Saloons were lavishly decorated in high Victorian style, but the cabins were still small. Charles Dickens, making the crossing in 1842, complained of his cabin, "I felt like a giraffe being persuaded into a flowerpot."[4]

Steamboats, flat-bottomed, shallow-draft craft that plied the inland rivers of the North American continent, developed on a track separate from but parallel to that of the grand steamships of the Atlantic.[5] Designed to carry cargo and passengers through the shifting shallows of the Ohio, Missouri, and Mississippi River systems, they became

Figure 81
Deluxe stateroom in first class, *MS Victoria,* Lloyd Triestino Line, operating between Italy and India in the 1930s.
Collection of Richard C. Faber, Jr., New York City.

the essential conduits of people and goods to the newly opening West. Sleeping conditions varied from a double brass bed in a stateroom equipped with private bath and washstand on the *J. M. White* *(fig. 80)* to the thoroughly uncomfortable accommodations described by John James Audubon aboard the *Gallant* in 1843: "My bed had two sheets, of course, measuring seven-eights of a yard wide; my pillow was filled with corn shucks. . . . our stateroom was evidently better fitted for the smoking of hams than the smoking of Christians."[6] Riverboats, although intended for carrying people from place to place, served far more consistently as work boats for cargo both human and material than for leisure travel.

The nineteenth-century drive toward progress and improvement, always undergirded by the desire for profit, brought rapid advances in steamship safety, comfort, and speed. British and German shipyards built ever larger ships, and with competition, the need for comfortable and even luxurious staterooms for first-class passengers grew. Ironically, the enormous profits made by the steamship lines were underwritten by millions of steerage passengers emigrating to North America. The *Kaiser Wilhelm der Grosse*, launched in 1897 by the North German Lloyd Line, had capacity for 558 first-class passengers, 338 second-class, and 1,074 in steerage.[7] European imperialist powers envisioned steamships connecting their empires, transporting raw materials extracted from the colonies back to Europe, and providing fast and easy journeys for administrators on their way to India, Africa, and elsewhere.

The interwar decades of the 1920s and 1930s were truly the heyday of luxury liners, which docked at ports all over the world. The open door to the United States had swung shut in 1921 with the American Quota Act, so ocean liners began catering to a different clientele, with first class, cabin class, and an improved third class. The confluence of comfort, affordability, and disposable income created the modern tourist and travel industry. The art deco aesthetic of clean lines and modern materials prevailed in ships built during this period *(fig. 81)*.

World War II changed everything. Not only was transatlantic travel extremely dangerous at that time, but each government commandeered ocean liners to serve as troop ships. The unprecedented use of airplanes in modern warfare naturally led to their

Figure 82
Pullman porter making up an upper berth aboard the *Capitol Limited*, bound for Chicago, Illinois, 1942.
Library of Congress. LC-USW3-000050.

increased use in peacetime. The luxury of six leisurely days crossing the Atlantic abruptly gave way to a six-hour commercial crossing by plane in 1958. Long-distance travel by ship withered and essentially died. In the 1960s, the grand shipping companies, such as Cunard and Holland America, transformed themselves from the transport business to the true leisure travel business—pleasure cruising.

Meanwhile, train travel followed a similar trajectory. From dirty, dangerous, uncomfortable journeys to transcontinental runs in ultimate luxury, long-distance train travel developed over the nineteenth and twentieth centuries only to be eclipsed by airplanes and automobiles in the 1960s. The steam engine that propelled the train was perfected in England, but American entrepreneurs later made refinements in passenger safety and comfort. The idea of a sleeping car percolated into many people's minds as early as the 1820s. No network of rails was yet in place to allow for such long-distance travel, but some visionaries recognized that the infrastructure would inevitably be built.[8] A number of individuals and companies in the United States worked at designing a car that would accommodate passengers more comfortably, with something other than the wooden benches then used as seats.[9]

The sleeping car as we imagine it—berths on either side, separated by curtains that were pulled at night—was manufactured by George M. Pullman outside Chicago *(fig. 82)*. The first version, although a tremendous improvement over the rudimentary planked bunks that some train lines supplied, was still not exactly luxurious. Sheets were not provided, and passengers had to be coerced into removing their shoes before climbing into a berth. An improved version of the Pullman Palace Car, called the Pioneer, made its commercial debut in 1867. The traveling public appreciated the elegant interior finishes, the new dining car, and the superb service rendered by conductors and porters. When the US transcontinental railroad was finished in 1869, Pullman was ready with the first coast-to-coast train in 1870. George Pullman owned no tracks or rail line himself; he sold first-class sleeping and dining cars to the railroads and offered his company's services to run them.

In Europe, the visionary Belgian engineer George Nagelmackers had a grand dream for a trans-European railway. Unsatisfied with the dormitory-style sleeping arrangements of the Pullman cars he had seen in the United States, he determined to devise the most comfortable, private, and luxurious accommodations possible for long-distance passengers.[10] He formed the *Compagnie Internationale des Wagon-Lits et des Grands Express Européens* to build sleeping and dining cars to cater to those who expected, and could afford, the best. Like Pullman, he owned no railways but wanted to supply the cars and profit from their use.

Europe's many national border crossings posed logistical problems for travelers. For a passenger to board a train and not have to remove luggage at each customs check would be a great improvement. Nagelmackers worked with the French rail line *Compagnie de l'Est* to put his new cars onto the newly planned long-distance express routes that were to cover the Continent. The most famous of these was the Paris-to-Istanbul run, dubbed the Orient Express. The first voyage of the Orient Express commenced at the *Gare de l'Est* in Paris on October 4, 1883. Big windows, modern gas lamps, a baggage car that could be checked by customs agents without disturbing the passengers, a lavish dining car equipped with a Burgundian chef, and two sleeping cars with private compartments that converted to two, three, or four berths guaranteed an exceptional journey to the dignitaries and journalists invited on board for the inaugural run. Subsequently, thousands of business and leisure travelers bought tickets with great anticipation.

Roomette

The Roomette pictured here, also designed for single occupancy, has the front edge of the folding type bed contoured at the lower end. Complete and private toilet facilities, ample luggage space, plenty of room for lounging and dressing, chilled drinking water and individual heat, light and air conditioning controls add to your comfort and enjoyment.

Day or night you are assured of complete privacy if that should be desired. In addition to the lights for general illumination, there also are reading and mirror lights for your individual control.

The bed when lowered for night use is over six feet long. It has a sleep inviting mattress and is pre-made with two pillows, crisp clean sheets and woolen blankets.

Careful pre-making of the bed adds to restful sleep.

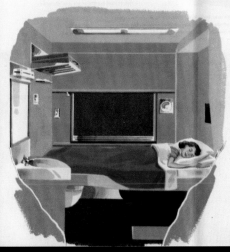

The wash basin is accessible, both day and night.

17

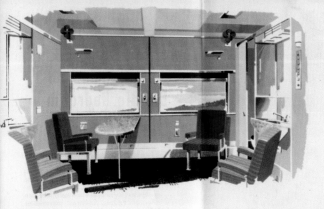

The bedroom suite, consisting of two connecting double bedrooms, appeals particularly to parents traveling with children. It is also favored by groups of business men who wish to have available en route a single large room for business conferences or social gatherings.

In nighttime use, the bedroom suite sleeps as many as four people with a separate bed for each. If less than four are to be accommodated, or if the party so prefers, the porter will be glad to prepare only the number and particular beds desired.

9

Figure 83
Advertising brochure,
Pullman sleeping cars, 1950.
Warburg Business Collection,
Archives Center, National Museum
of American History, Smithsonian
Institution.

All over the world, imperial powers were building railroads to bring goods to market, transport administrators and emigrants, and encourage the burgeoning tourism industry. Burton Holmes, the famous American traveler and lecturer, wrote of his journey on the Trans-Siberian Railroad in 1901 that "the compartments are extremely comfortable. They are arranged on the plan of the Mann Boudoir cars, with berths across the car instead of up and down the sides. The upper berth is raised during the day, leaving a divan where we may sit to read or lie to doze."[11] The Trans-Siberian, with its various branches and spurs, linked Moscow with the Pacific port of Vladivostock, with Beijing, and with the wilds of Mongolia. The British built thousands of miles of track in India, less in Africa. Train travel was at its height into the first decades of the twentieth century.

The shift to diesel engines in the 1930s made the new streamlined trains quieter and cleaner. The marriage of form and function that industrial designers brought to

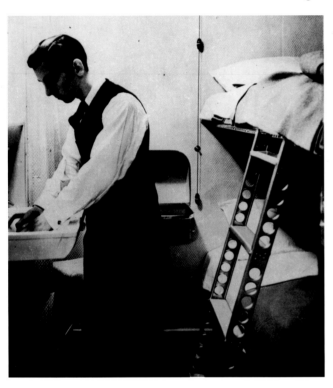

Figure 84
Unidentified man washing his hands in the sink in a cabin of the German airship LZ 129 *Hindenburg*.
National Air and Space Museum, Smithsonian Institution, SI 77-8277.

Figure 85
Breakfast in bed aboard a United Airlines Douglas DST (Douglas Sleeper Transport), c. 1936.
United Airlines photograph, National Air and Space Museum, Smithsonian Institution, SI 2005-22907.

the design and manufacture of these new trains engendered an exciting, dynamic period of train travel. For the first time in railroad history the look of a train was integrated throughout the engine and the cars. Color schemes, the innovative use of metals and woods for trim, and interior appointments together created a unified look that reflected the line's "personality" as well as the specific route the train serviced. The Union Pacific's *City of Denver* included the "Frontier Shack" lounge, which evoked the Old West with the use of rough wood, log beams, and stuffed animal heads, while the Atchison, Topeka & Santa Fe's *Super Chief* realized a Southwest Indian theme.[12] Sleeping accommodations on these new trains were varied and flexible. From "roomettes" for one to three-person drawing rooms and adjoining bedrooms that could be combined into larger rooms, they accommodated all manner of travelers *(fig. 83)*.

Pullman continued to build cars to the specifications of railroad company designers during this era of stylish train travel and on until 1981. The rise of the automobile for commuting and the airplane for long-distance travel seriously hurt the rail industry in the

United States following World War II. Train travel and manufacturing innovation have remained alive in Europe, but in the United States Amtrak, born in 1971 to rescue what remained of private passenger transport, has struggled with variable ridership and the reluctance of travelers to spend time in this age of jet speed. Sleeper cars are still available to those who have that luxury.

Air travel is the bane of a good night's sleep in the twenty-first century, but it was not always so. The first passenger-carrying, nonstop Atlantic crossings by air were made by those elegant airships called dirigibles.[13] In 1919, a British-made airship called the R.34 crossed from Scotland to New York in four and a half days. The interwar period saw the development of these lighter-than-air ships and their use for intercontinental travel. In the 1930s, travel time between Germany and New York was reduced to three days. Passengers slept in tiny cabins—only 78 inches long by 66 inches wide (198 by 167.5 cm)—which held two berths, a folding washstand, and a collapsible writing table

(fig. 84). Passengers spent most of their time in the lounge, looking out the windows. Dirigible flights across the Atlantic, landing in the United States and Brazil, ended with the disaster of the *Hindenburg*, which exploded on May 6, 1937, killing thirty-five of the ninety-seven persons on board. Growing political tensions contributed to the difficulty of ensuring passengers' safety in these helium-filled ships. Commercial air travel was destined to evolve from the heavier-than-air planes that were developing simultaneously.

Figure 86
Green Tortoise bus interior.

The history of commercial long-distance flight in airplanes is again one of dead ends, arduous manufacturing developments, and singular personalities.[14] By the 1930s, transcontinental flights carried passengers and mail around Europe and North America. But long-distance, nonstop flights were not yet possible. Early planes could not carry enough fuel to cross an ocean without stopping to refuel. Transpacific flights made in flying boats—aircraft that landed on water and loaded passengers from a dock—hopped from California to Manila and Hong Kong via Hawaii, Midway, and Guam. The Boeing 314 called the *Yankee Clipper,* which flew Pan Am's North Atlantic route to Europe, was launched in 1939 and had sleeping berths for thirty-six passengers. Interior photographs show a remarkable likeness to train décor of the time. Meanwhile, United Airlines was using the DST—Douglas Sleeper Transport, later known as the DC3—for transcontinental flights *(fig. 85).*

World War II put a hold on commercial aviation but also necessitated the building of infrastructure such as airports and long runways so that giant planes could fly around the world. The 1960s saw the popularization of long-distance air travel—once a privilege of the wealthy—through the creation of different classes of service that offered differing amenities for a price. Economy class was born, with passengers packed in like sardines, and the possibility of comfortably sleeping while traveling was again limited to the first-class few.

Airlines and airplane manufacturers work in tandem to design the interior space in a plane. In some first-class cabins, seats that fold down to a fully flat surface are making a comeback, as in the Airbus 320 series. New, ever larger planes are being designed with the possibility of sleeper cabins and a return to the luxury of space, for those who can afford the ticket.[15]

Figure 87
Peter Marlow, On the train to
Coney Island.
New York, 2001.

Travelers on the other end of the financial spectrum have little opportunity to sleep. Long-distance bus transport has to be the most uncomfortable option available for getting from one place to another. In the early 1970s, two entrepreneurs started alternative bus companies—the Green Tortoise and the Grey Rabbit. They bought old buses and remodeled them into long-distance sleeping coaches. In the early years the accommodations were funky, with foam mattresses on the floor and webbing bunks suspended from the ceilings. Today, Green Tortoise still operates—more as a tour company offering low-cost adventure travel than as a long-distance transport company, but the premise is the same. Updated and slightly less communal, berths hang from the ceiling, and booths and couches that convert into beds make for comfortable, budget-conscious sleeping on the road *(fig. 86)*.

Notes

1. This is not to say that no one traveled for pleasure or curiosity before Europeans started wandering the globe. Arabs, for example, have a long history of travel and discovery, beginning with voyages to the European and African continents in the eleventh century and documentation in the form of geographies. With the improvement of roads and security in eighteenth-century England, the wealthiest Britons began shuttling around their own country and the Continent. Popular leisure travel can be said to have started in the late nineteenth century with the invention of the steamship, the steamboat, and the railroad sleeper car.

2. Quoted in Stephen Fox, *Transatlantic: Samuel Cunard, Isambard Brunel, and the Great Atlantic Steamships* (New York: HarperCollins, 2003), 11.

3. *The Savannah,* an American-owned ship, used a steam engine and paddlewheel to assist its sails in a crossing from Savannah to Ireland in 1819. Fox, *Transatlantic,* 73.

4. Quoted in Bill Miller, *Ocean Liners: Travel on the Open Sea* (New York: Mallard Press, 1990), 11.

5. Harry Sinclair Drago, *The Steamboaters: From the Early Side-Wheelers to the Big Packets* (New York: Dodd, Mead, 1967).

6. John James Audubon, *The Audubon Journals,* vol. 1 (Boston: Charles Scribners Sons, 1897), 450–451, quoted in Drago, *Steamboaters,* 19.

7. Miller, *Ocean Liners,* 17-18. According to Miller, more than 12 million people crossed the Atlantic in third class or steerage between 1900 and 1914.

8. Stewart H. Holbrook, *The Story of American Railroads* (New York: Crown, 1947).

9. Mann's Boudoir Cars, the Flower Sleeping Car, and the Wagner Palace Car Company, among others, all manufactured sleeping cars and were all eventually bought or put out of business by Pullman.

10. Gary Hogg, *Orient Express: The Birth, Life, and Death of a Great Train* (New York: Walker, 1968), 15.

11. Burton Holmes, *The Burton Holmes Lectures,* vol. 8 (Battle Creek, MI: Little-Preston Company, 1901), 241–246 (available online at www.TravelHistory.org).

12. Bob Johnston, Joe Welsh, and Mike Schafer, *The Art of the Streamliner* (New York: Metro Books, 2001).

13. *Dirigible* came from the French word *diriger,* "to steer." Airships with rigid frames were also called zeppelins, after Ferdinand Graf von Zeppelin, their German builder and promoter. A blimp is a large, steerable gas balloon with suspended passenger car and tail fin.

14. For a detailed account, see Tom D. Crouch, *Wings: A History of Aviation from Kites to the Space Age* (New York: W. W. Norton, 2003).

15. For instance, Airbus announced in January 2005 that the 380 series would offer two decks with flexible space that could be configured as the customer desired. Ever larger airplanes seem to be on the horizon.

6. Sleeping in the Modern World

"When I sleep I sleep and do not dream because it is as well that I am what I seem when I am in my bed and dream." —*Gertrude Stein*

Annie Carlano

Sleeping in the Modern World

In Great Britain, ideas, styles, and fashions concerning the bed changed little from medieval times until the second half of the nineteenth century. By the 1860s, materials and designs had begun to change, driven from one direction by new medical findings about the unhygienic nature of the four-poster, with its insect-infested wood and stifling draperies, and, from another direction, by the artistic disaster of the 1851 Exhibition of the Art and Industry of All Nations. Commonly referred to as the Great Exhibition, this watershed in design history was a crowd pleaser, showcasing the largest display of home furnishings ever, but also a testament to an overabundance of outmoded, bad design.[1]

Charles Eastlake's influential book *Hints on Household Taste in Furniture, Upholstery and Other Details,* first published in London in 1868, advocated the simplification of interior design. Eastlake sided with the health reformers and sought to free

Figure 88
Jane Morris's bedroom at Kelmscott Manor, Gloucestershire, with fabrics and wallpaper by her husband, William Morris.

Figure 89
Iron bedstead with canopy, designed by Charles L. Eastlake.
From his *Hints on Household Taste in Furniture, Upholstery and Other Details,* 1878.

Figure 90
Murphy-in-a-door hideaway
bed on view at the Vonnegut
Hardware booth at the
Hardware Home Show Display,
1925.
Bass Photo Company Collection,
Indiana Historical Society.

the bedroom from its unhealthy trappings. Bemoaning the prevalence of frilly, overdeco-
rated bedrooms at the time, he wrote: "Somehow, in the midst of lace bed curtains,
muslin toilet covers, pink calico, and cheval glasses, one might fancy oneself in a
milliner's shop." He believed that "a room intended for repose should contain nothing
which can fatigue the eye."

Yet even among the enlightened, modernity met resistance. Eastlake acknowledged that it was more wholesome to sleep on a metal bedstead, but he found it
ludicrous to suggest that bed curtains were inherently stifling and harbored germs.
Taking matters literally into his own hands, he created the design shown in figure 89,
to demonstrate how beautiful an iron bed with a canopy and hangings could be.

Among other people who wrote about beds and bedrooms, Lady Barker, a
world traveler, offered a candid look into the intimate details of things such as mattresses, noting that the most unsanitary ones were not those of far-off lands but those
of Britain. Topping her list of unhealthy sleeping surfaces were mattresses filled with
lumpy natural wool and chopped grass, a "stinky feather bed in Scotland," and a

seaweed mattress—equally pungent, one imagines—in an Irish hotel.² Although Lady Barker agreed that metal bedsteads were more hygienic than wooden ones, she offered illustrations of both in her book and recommended going to the Royal School of Needlework for bed hangings and hanging one's walls with pretty stretched chintzes.³ Eastlake had noted earlier, however, that the quality of furnishing textiles had degenerated to the point that both craftsmanship and design were at an all-time low.⁴

William Morris, Eastlake's contemporary, took care of that. Leading the way from the retardataire neo-Gothic through aestheticism to the progressive Arts and Crafts movement, he created textile designs that were startlingly new and beautiful. With their inspiration in the finely woven tapestries of the Middle Ages, Indo-Persian silks, and other "pre-Raphael" patterns, these designs went beyond historical rehashing and into the contemporary world. Reflecting Morris's keen social concern for beauty in utilitarian objects for all classes and his passion for the natural world of flowers and birds, the fabrics he designed and produced for his own bed and those of his family were particularly popular and remain design classics (fig. 88).

What Morris contributed to the modernization of the bed was brilliant: fabrics for bed hangings and windows that were at once hygienic and attractive, made of lightweight cotton, not heavy wool or silk damask, and all hand blocked, printed, and embroidered. Through his firm, Morris and Company, en suite wallpapers were also available, as seen in

Figure 91
A closed Murphy bed in a Chicago loft.
Architect Ed Noonan, 2004.

figure 88. Opening the door to modernity, Morris led the way for Voysey, Mackintosh and the "Glasgow girls," and M. H. Baillie Scott, whose interior schemes always included furnishing fabrics with images of the natural world, such as a green coverlet with a variety of wildflowers, suggesting that one was lying on a meadow in one's bed. Baillie Scott described the room in which this coverlet dominated the color scheme as "while not aggressively sanitary, one hopes [it] might lead to pleasant dreaming."⁵

Arts and Crafts bedsteads, in Britain and the United States, were, despite the fad for metal beds, usually massive oak constructions, destined for relatively large-scale bedrooms. But in the first decades of the twentieth century, most of the population was grappling with how to live comfortably in the modern small-scale apartment. Affordable and healthy, beds of iron or brass, sometimes combined with wooden elements, were to be found on both sides of the Atlantic, from the servants' quarters of grand country homes to middle-class row houses. In hospitals and in "sick rooms"—separate bedrooms for isolating those who were ill—metal beds prevailed. In cities and rural areas,

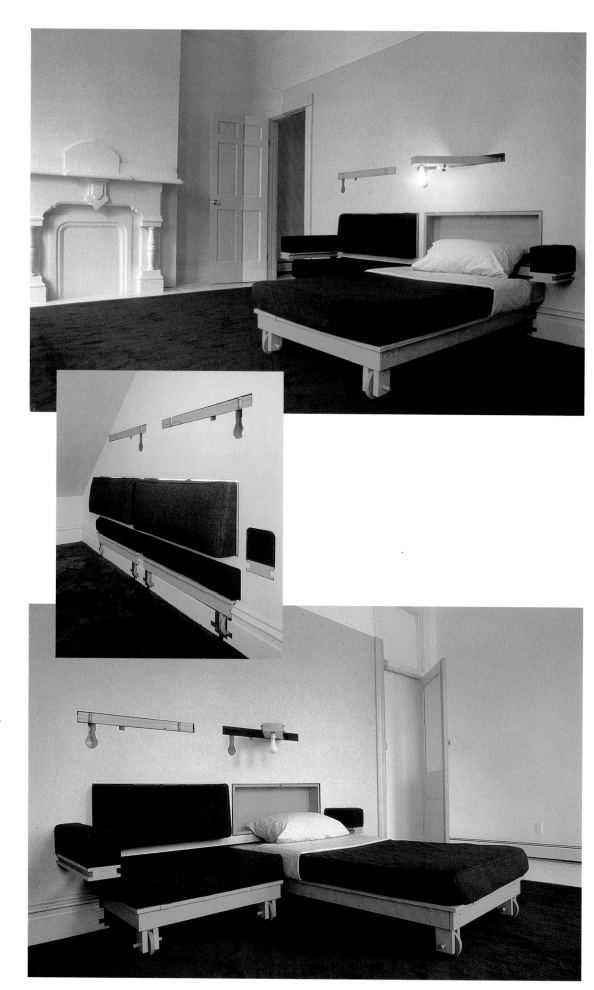

Figure 92
Living quarters for the
Mattress Factory Gallery
residence, three views.
Designer Allan Wexler, 1988.

these mass-produced factory beds were available for sleepers of all ages in the form of singles, doubles, cribs, and even space-saving collapsibles, an example of which was recently offered for sale on eBay.[6]

The Murphy bed *(fig. 90)*, a hideaway, mechanized version of the European press bed, was a further space-saving design invented in the early 1900s by the Californian William L. Murphy, who sought a way to accommodate a larger bed for himself and his new wife in a one-room San Francisco apartment.[7] Without posts, and therefore without a canopy, it was the vanguard of the minimalist bedstead. Leading designers incorporated hideaway beds into affluent urban interiors. An example is the architect Erno Goldfinger's 1939 bed for a small bedroom in his Hampstead house; it could be tipped up to be stowed away à la Murphy. Satisfying both the need for more space and the desire for a fashionable, modern interior design, the Murphy bed

continues to be relevant in the twenty-first century. In 2004, for example, in architecturally forward Chicago, the architect Ed Noonan, at the request of art collectors Eugenie and Lael Johnson, creatively incorporated a Murphy bed into the design for a den in their loft in a renovated River North building *(fig. 91)*.

Beyond innovations in bed design, modern design solutions for sleeping in small spaces included radical changes to interior architecture. Foremost of these was the open plan created by the Dutch designer and architect Gerrit Rietveld. The house he designed for Mrs. Truus Schröder-Schräder and her three children in Utrecht in 1926 is the first example of an open-plan interior design. Upstairs, the children's sleeping quarters were defined not by walls but by partitions. Reitveld developed this concept so that the children would have private bedrooms at night but a large play space by day. In 1988, Allan Wexler took both the idea of the Murphy bed and the concept of an open plan further when he designed the living quarters for an artist in residence at the Mattress Factory: he invented a bed that could be moved through either side of a wall, depending on where the occupant needed it *(fig. 92)*. In his 1991 *Crate House*, an entire bedroom is broken down into its basic components and contained in a crate on wheels *(fig. 93)*.

Figure 93
Allan Wexler,
Crate House, 1991.
Bedroom, wood and mixed media,
80 x 60 x 30 in. (203.2 x 152.4 x 76.2 cm).

Another space-saving design with roots in earlier mechanical contraptions is the sofa bed. Its dual nature, "sofa" and "bed," is cleverly disguised by the upholstery fabric or slipcover. Seating furniture by day and sleeping furniture by night, this twentieth-century object was coveted by Americans just entering the middle class after the Second World War and furnishing their newly built tract houses in affordable developments such as Levittown, New York. In homes with several children and no rooms to spare, sofa beds gave suburbanites a place to sleep the occasional house guest. In the New York City metropolitan area during the late 1960s and 1970s, print and television ads for "Castro convertibles" were ubiquitous—it seemed everyone was singing the jingle.

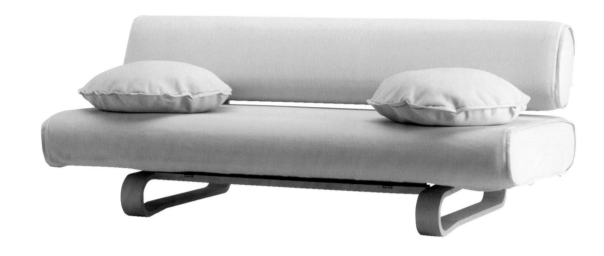

"One out of every six Europeans

Figure 94
Selection of IKEA sofa beds
from the company's online
catalog, 2006.

sleep on an IKEA bed"

Today, many furniture manufacturers worldwide produce these now common-place objects, and most middle-class home furnishing companies feature a variety of styles in their mail-order catalogs, on their websites, and in their stores. From Sears to Target, budget shoppers can find a range of sleeper sofas to satisfy their traditional or trendy design preferences. Stealing the market in Europe, where the equivalent of the Castro convertible advertising campaign is the "one out of six Europeans sleeps on an IKEA bed" mantra, that Swedish firm has provided a hip range of sofa bed designs at remarkably low prices for several decades *(fig. 94)*.

As cultural mores changed radically in the second half of the twentieth century, new types of beds appeared, their designs reinventing their function. In the 1960s, the youth-centered society of "sex, drugs, and rock and roll"—and politics—proclaimed its unabashed promiscuity with slogans such as "make love not war." Embracing nature, hippies needed only the soft earth or a mattress in a van as a bed. Catering in part to this new sexual freedom, but also to the classic pursuit of a better night's sleep, the modern water bed appeared in 1969 and was soon adapted to a variety of contemporary styles.[8] Editorial cartoons humorously compared its liberal appeal to the attraction old-fashioned canopy beds held for the more conservative consumer *(fig. 95)*. Is it any wonder that this sensuous aquatic bed was created and first enjoyed in San Francisco, the epicenter of the American counterculture revolution?

Figure 95
Cartoon illustrating generational differences in sleeping styles, New York, 1960s.

The bed functioned as a political tool in 1969 when John Lennon and Yoko Ono staged a "bed-in" for peace. Combining the intellectual tenacity of the sit-in with the emotional euphoria of the love-in, they used their celebrity to focus world attention on nonviolent alternatives to war. Staying in bed for a week soon after their marriage, first at the Amsterdam Hilton and then at the Queen Elizabeth Hotel in Montreal, Lennon and Ono, not unlike the Sun King and Madame, engaged in often heated discussions with visitors at their contemporary *levée*. Their hotel beds were luxurious versions of the typical reduced bedstead of the time, with neither headboard nor footboard *(fig. 96)*.[9]

The reductive, minimalist bed of the late 1960s and 1970s was a result of both the pervading aesthetic of art and design and the younger generation's interest in world or ethnic culture, as manifested in part by the popular phenomenon of backpacking treks to foreign lands. Rejecting the elaborate, bourgeois bedsteads of their parents, the counterculture, identifying with people in non-Western societies, pulled the mattress off the bed and plunked it defiantly on the floor *(fig. 97)*. Proponents of minimalism in the design world lauded the pared-down, tranquil beauty of both Japanese tatami and futon and Shaker wooden bedsteads.[10] Some time later, in 1987, when the architect and design guru Bernard Rudofsky curated the *Sparta/Sybaris* exhibition at the Museum für Angewandte Kunst in Vienna, his ideal sleeping room was portrayed as a Japanese-style tatami and enclosed futon. Rudofsky saw this type of bedding, in its portability and poetry, as what we would today call better feng shui, the form most suitable for healthy

Figure 97
Baron Wolman, Musician Jeff
Beck sleeping on a motel bed
mattress on the floor, 1968.

Figure 98
Baron Wolman, Janis Joplin
on her bed in Haight-Ashbury,
San Francisco, 1967.

sleeping.[11] Simple bedsteads or mattresses on the floor were often covered, paradoxically, with intricately patterned bedcovers or tribal rugs. Printed cottons from India, available at patchouli-scented "head shops," were the mass-market wall hangings and bedcovers of choice *(fig. 98)*. Eventually, counterculture bedding preferences influenced high style, sparking trends such as "ethnic style," "Moroccan style," and "Caribbean style."

Fabrics, as they had for centuries, once again defined the bed in the 1960s and 1970s. The burgeoning interest in world textiles and the flowering of the Arts and Crafts movement caused Americans to see the quilt not as just a sentimental relic of times past but as something wonderfully handmade and colorful with which to decorate their beds. Quilt making, along with other needlecrafts of the grandmothers, such as crocheting, knitting, and macramé, underwent a renaissance, bringing a new Romantic, if not precisely neo-Victorian, feeling to the bed and boudoir. The kaleidoscope of colors and optical patterns found in some historic American quilts appealed to, and inspired, contemporary psychedelic graphic style *(fig. 99)*.

Figure 99
American bedroom in warm
shades of red and gold.
McCall's Needlework and Crafts,
Fall–Winter 1967–1968.

The Finnish firm Marimekko developed brightly colored, bold stripes and large floral blossom patterns to be screen-printed on bedding for goose-feather duvets, mattresses, and pillows, defining features of the modern Scandinavian bed in the 1970s *(fig. 100)*. Youthful and exuberant, these fabrics were the center of attention, hiding the platform teak or painted wood frame. The platform bed with its duvet was both hip in its minimalism, eliminating layers of sheets and blankets, headboard and footboard, and practical, sometimes harboring storage areas inside and bookshelves at its sides.

Several great American studio furniture artists gained prominence at this time, including George Nakashima, Timothy Simpson, and Sam Maloof. Admiring the achievements of Wharton Esherick and seeking to return to the Arts and Crafts tenet of beautiful handmade furniture for everyone, they heeded the "back to the garden" self-sufficiency call of the flower children. Woodworkers began to make furniture for their own homes and those of others. Maloof's cradle *(fig. 101)*, featured in the 1966 exhibition *The Bed* at the Museum of Contemporary Crafts, is a good example of a finely handcrafted domestic utilitarian object with no extraneous decoration. Two contemporary furniture makers carrying on this woodworking tradition are James Schriber and Charles Durfee, while Wendy Maruyama's bed designs are more "pop" commentaries and autobiographies *(fig. 102)*.[12]

The London architect and designer—and restaurateur—Terence Conran initiated the democratization of trendy contemporary design in home furnishings through the stores Conran Shops and Habitat, which he established in London and abroad in the 1960s.[13] On the other side of the pond, Conran clones such as Crate and Barrel and Pottery Barn opened, catering to American tastes by offering furniture and other items in a more understated vein. Comfort and cocooning were reflected in the bedroom vignettes set up in shop windows and store displays, where styles from Ralph Lauren–inspired country overstuffed to the more urban duvet-covered "bed-in-a-minute" were put into the context of room as womb.

Figure 100
Platform bed with bedding in
a pattern called "Menuetti,"
by Anneli Qveflander for
Marimekko, 1968.

Martha Stewart, sensing the growing desire on the part of affluent young Americans to create cozy nests around 1980, offered them entire lifestyles through her books, magazine, and television programs. Comfort food and antique home furnishings were her domains. To adorn that New England four-poster, she recommended a sumptuous variety of pristine bedcovers, from candlewick spreads, Bates of Maine novelty covers, and machine-woven "Marseilles" quilts to that item ever evocative of baby boomer childhood, the chenille spread *(fig. 103)*. The democratization of Martha Stewart designs was born with her line of bedding for Kmart in 1997 and the diaspora of other brand-name, lifestyle bed linens, coverlets, and beds, all within the push of the television remote control in the cable kingdoms of QVC and the Home Shopping Network.

Tot and teen bed designs, too, became increasingly creative.[14] The basic forms of cradle, bassinet, crib, twin bed, bunk bed, and trundle bed endured but were animated by fashionable styles for wee ones as well as advances in pediatrics. Boomer-generation parents and yuppies alike wanted their children to reflect their station in life, dressing and housing them to the best of their ability and following the latest word in prenatal care and postpartum practices. For infants, the trademarked Snugli allowed moms, dads, and caretakers to keep infants close to their heartbeats and promote sleep. Parents were often inventive themselves, as in Jim and Joan Wright's "boy nest," a single duvet used as a feather-bed for their young son Benjamin. In 2002, Pamela and Richard Fogel purchased the new "co-sleeper" so that baby Helene could breast-feed in bed.

Figure 101
Sam Maloof, cradle, 1966.
Walnut.
48 x 30 x 36 in.
(121.9 x 76.2 x 91.4 cm).
Collection of Mr. and Mrs. Maynard Orme.

Figure 103
Vintage bedspreads.
Martha Stewart Living,
June 2003.

Children's bedrooms began to be taken as serious design projects in the Peter Pan culture of the 1960s. A generation of parents who wanted never to grow up enjoyed reveling in the needs of their offspring. To indulge both parents and children, architects, academics, and artists throughout the international design world, from Marimekko in Finland and Design Research in the United States to Takashimaya in Japan, created strikingly inventive designs. Newfangled bunk beds might have stairways to play areas and reading lofts, along with fantastical fabrics and wall decorations. Kids' bedrooms became multipurpose living spaces in the affluent 1980s, serving not merely as a playroom–sleep room but also, with the advent of the "computer for every child" culture, as cyber central.

Camouflaged by the usual detritus of toys, games, clothes, and coverlets, the sleeping surface of the preteen or adolescent seems to be the least important piece of furniture in the room as the activity of sleep loses its appeal during these years—until one attempts to wake the child up and get him or her ready for school, at which point hibernation sets in. Yet sleeping outside the bedroom, escaping the confines of deco-

Figure 105
Madonna performing on a
brass bed, March 18, 1995.

Figure 106
Children at a *soirée pyjama*,
suburban Paris, France,
2004.

rum—from sacking out in tents or teepees in the backyard in sleeping bags (whether the authentic camping type from the sporting goods store or the Hollywood version featuring the current most popular superhero) to dragging an air mattress into the den for an all-night DVD marathon appeals to a boy's sense of the wild and crazy.

Girls, meanwhile, tend to crave the more social pajama party, also known as the slumber party or sleepover *(fig. 104)*. More about intimacy and giggles than adventure, they might find preteens and teens lounging indoors on the most fashionable portable sleeping surfaces, such as the inflatable "ready bed," a sleeping bag and air mattress in one, featuring pop culture motifs such as Disney Princess, Barbie, Hello Kitty, and Spiderman. Many grown-up American girls still cherish the memories of their slumber parties; some even hold reunions. Others, capitalizing on the sleepover's metaphors and innuendos, use it to catch our attention. Madonna, for one, sat on an old-fashioned brass bed in her 1995 *Bedtime Story* video, which MTV aired to millions worldwide *(fig. 105)*.[15]

In Paris, where the *soirée pyjama*, or sleepover party, more regularly features boys and girls, it may actually take place in a bedroom, as at the home of Antoine Lorgnier and Agnes Fruman *(fig. 106)*.

Here, one notes the pervasive Asian aesthetic, both in the form of the platform bed and in the bedding, which features Japanese-printed cotton pillowcases and a futon cover over the duvet.[16] The bottom sheet, however, is a plain white handspun linen antique from the Clignancourt flea market. Since the seventeenth century the French have had a penchant for seamlessly fusing Asian and European design traditions to create a harmonious elegance, a result of both their history and their taste.

Bedrooms in university housing have gone from the neo-monastic modernism of Alvar Aalto's interiors for the Massachusetts Institute of Technology in 1946–1948 to the exuberant self-decorated dorm rooms of today. Students at the Rhode Island School of Design (RISD) and the Pratt Institute of Design, the future style creators of tomorrow, show us what might be ahead in bed design *(figs. 107 and 108)*. A postmodern eclecticism can be seen in the footboard in figure 108, which is both concealed and punctuated by being wrapped in a synthetic industrial material, and in the bold geometric graphics of the fabrics and the use of recycled decorating materials in figure 107. Off campus, young people, newlyweds, and others starting out or starting over can choose from a plethora of bed designs to find the one that best suits their personality and style. In a "me" driven culture, the perfect bedroom is one that speaks of the occupants' needs, tastes, and worldview. Health-conscious, cutting-edge, or traditional—anything goes. And when the cover of a mainstream decorating magazine features a look inside top interior designers' homes, with four radically different bedrooms, it seems that "high" and "low" have converged, and the elite and the ethnic hold equal interest.[17]

Figure 107
Dorm room of Greer Marx Goodman, 29, and Lucy Stamper, 27. M.S. in interior design, class of 2005, Pratt Institute of Design.

Figure 108
Dorm room of Lauren Jenison, 21. B.F.A. in textiles, class of 2005, Rhode Island School of Design.

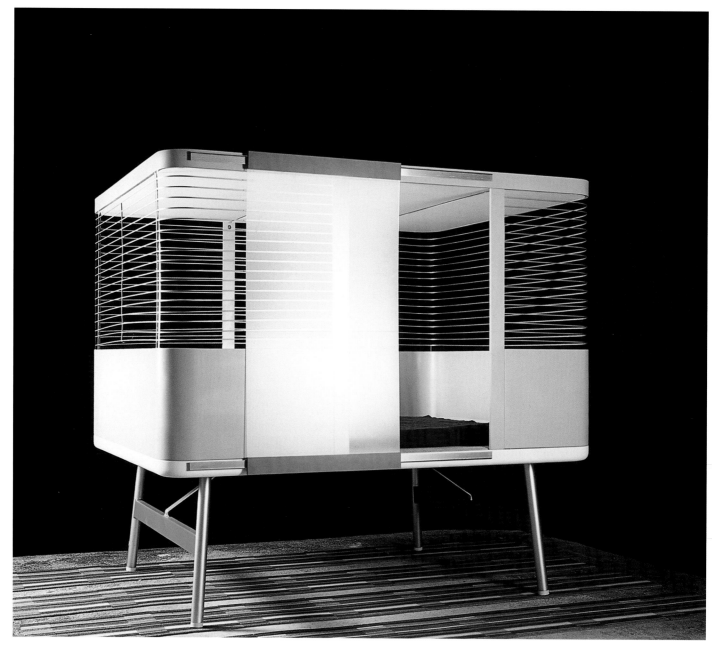

Figure 109
Ronan and Erwan Bouroullec,
Lit clos, produced by
Cappellini, 2000.
Painted birch plywood, steel,
aluminum, altuglas,
78¾ x 94½ x 55¼ in.
(200 x 240 x 140 cm).

There are always exceptions. Since the 1960s, when Germany's *über* Ulm design school proclaimed that functionalism and rationalism were obsolete—a perspective that spread throughout the international design community—artist- and architect-conceived sleeping surfaces and bedrooms have become more imaginative, drawing on popular culture and scientific breakthroughs in materials, chiefly plastics, and processes, such as molding. Claes Oldenburg's 1963 *Bedroom Ensemble*, a playful commentary on the artificiality of Western culture, contained a bed and other furniture covered in slick shiny synthetics. Archizoom's 1967 *Rosa Imperiale* and Joe Colombo's 1971 *Closing Bed*, both for the furniture company Sormani, and Michael Graves's 1981 bedroom furniture for the avant-garde design firm Memphis all speak with an over-the-top optimism to an audience happy to discard the notion that form must follow function and to embrace anarchy. In the postmodern era, when no one philosophy or sensibility informs the most brilliant designers of our times and no startling new theory has been offered about the nature of sleep, innovation in bed design is elusive. Nonetheless, several international designers have grappled with the conundrum of the bed form successfully, albeit quite differently.

The French designers and brothers Erwan and Ronan Bouroullec have created objects and furniture together since 1999. Familiar with the form of the historic *lit clos* (see chapter 3) of their native Quimper, and recognizing the utility of such a design in cold climates, they sought to reinvent the concept for contemporary life *(fig. 109)*. Unlike the heavy wooden rustic designs of the earlier types, their *lit clos* is a lightweight metal and synthetic sleeping chamber. Shaped somewhat like a 1960s television console, it is a room within a room, providing privacy and a sense of escape from normal life as well as insulation from the cold.[18]

Derin, a father-and-son furniture company based in Istanbul, is one design firm whose creations represent a return to the sedate functionalism of modernist prototypes *(figs. 110 and 111)*. Their beds are superb examples of what the Danish chair designer and critic Hans J. Wegner defined as good design: "True design asks one thing of us, to uncover what it covers."[19] Going beyond the mere straightforward, their beds are objects of beauty, exhibiting colors, textures, and lines that are pleasingly seductive. They intrigue us with their sleek modernity and their historicism, speaking vaguely of ancient Stoic bedsteads.

When rock legend Lou Reed wanted furniture for his New York loft, he turned to the artist cum industrial chic designer Jim Zivic. Trained as a painter and sculptor, Zivic has an innate sensitivity to what he has described as "masculine" materials. Raw steel, rough aluminum, and hot zinc exemplify his predilection for metal. He and Reed collaborated on designs for the loft space, including the paradoxically lyrical daybed shown in figure 112.[20]

Harvard's Graduate School of Design presented its first award for design excellence to Philippe Starck in 1997. Hearing him talk about his work in a slide presentation in which he showed familiar architectural projects and whimsical kitchen items for the Italian design company Alessi, I was struck by the more intimate images from his own home. Starck's penchant for domestic design is nowhere more evident than in the bedrooms he has designed for hotels worldwide, including one of his first, for the Paramount Hotel in New York City *(fig. 113)*. Neo-pop yet unmistakably Starck, this bed is a statement about our complex needs *au lit* today. We sleep in bed, make love in bed, watch TV or DVDs with family in bed; we eat breakfast and, in the case of hotels, other room-service meals in bed, as we recline or sit up with the help of ample pillows. Starck's bed for the vacationer or business traveler is equipped to meet all these needs with its comfortable elegance and urbane art allusions.

The Milanese design company Flou, whose subtitle-slogan, "La Cultura del Dormire," means "sleep culture," has occupied a supreme niche since 1978 as a think tank of cutting-edge science and art concerning the bed. Studying the different phases of sleep, the dangers of stress, and the "rules" of a good sleep—the quality of sleep vis-à-vis the specifics of the mattress, pillows (some of which are filled with corn fiber), and duvets—Flou offers advice in words and furniture. Approaching each client/patient as an individual, its philosophy is that each person is different and requires a specific type of bed in order to sleep well and thereby be happier. To achieve their design goals, Flou's staff members work with Italy's most talented designers and architects. Experimenting with new materials, they develop products of technical innovation and fine quality, from fabrics to metals.

Figure 110
Plain,
designed by Studio Derin,
2002, for Derin Design.

Figure 111
Mild,
designed by Studio Derin,
2003, for Derin Design.

Figure 112
Jim Zivic,
daybed for Lou Reed's
New York loft, 2004.

Enzo Mari's *Tappeto volante* (flying carpet) is a Flou classic *(fig. 114)*. It features an iron bedstead that can be constructed in a number of ways and a mattress support that can be made of wooden slats or an electro-soldered grille. It has two interchangeable bed heads, one large semicircular one or two small ones. The semicircular bed head can be padded with a Flou fabric or not, the height of the bed can be adjusted, and the wall behind the bed can be customized with a Flou tapestry.

Exploration and new designs are constants at Flou, whose 2005 beds included Mario Bellini's *Marilyn*, Operadesign's *Harris Bed*, and two by Rodolfo Dordoni, *Plaza* and *You & Me*. At the same time, the vibrancy and timelessness of beds created years ago, such as *Tappeto volante* and Vico Magistretti's *Nathalie*, are apparent in their continued desirability.

Bill Murray's character in the 2003 film *Lost in Translation* spends a lot of screen time on his king-size bed in his spacious hotel bedroom in the real-life Tokyo Park Hyatt. A Japanese hotel for Westerners, its design differs radically from those created exclusively for the Japanese, among whom short, narrow beds are still the norm. And although Murray's room seems to Western eyes to be very Zenlike, its large elevated bed is a far cry from the way most Japanese today sleep—still in the traditional way, in small spaces, on the tatami and futon and behind the shoji.[21]

Art imitates life. In a photograph by Dore Gardner *(fig. 115)*, her father sits on the edge of a vast terrain of bed, lost in his emptiness. Here, as in director Sofia Coppola's scene in *Lost in Translation*, the bed, the symbol of life, is an active part of the narrative, conveying through style and lack of occupancy a sense of sadness and alienation.

Today, sleeping often gets short shrift. Insomnia plagues us. Illness strikes. Our busy schedules keep us awake and out of bed, to the detriment of our work life. Noting this cultural phenomenon, Dorothy Meade offered this "Bed-side Kit for Insomniacs":

Figure 113
Bedroom in the Paramount
Hotel, New York,
designed by Philippe Starck,
1991.

Fly swat: for nocturnal insects
Wedges: for rattling windows
Jug of water: for courting cats and passers-by
who make remotely cat-like noises
Blindfold: to keep out light
Earplugs: for irrepressible noises
Notebook and pencil: for scintillating early-hour
ideas
Volume of Encyclopaedia Britannica (or sleeping
pet): to anchor slipping bed clothes
Snacks: for night starvation
Sponge: to silence dripping taps till the new
washer is fixed
A boring book

Getting out of bed is the only cure for: worry about all the things you ought to have done (do some of them); badly made bed; crumbs between the sheets; burst hot water bottle (total remake); children snuggling into your bed (they must be led gently back into their own—unless you pretend you haven't noticed)
Less tangible causes are the province of doctors and drugs[22]

Two young adrenaline-active entrepreneurs, Christopher Lindholst and Arshad Chowdhury, started a company called MetroNaps in New York in 2003. Based in the Empire State Building in mid-town Manhattan, MetroNaps gives sleep-deprived workers a chance to catch a few winks on their lunch hour and return to work refreshed. Napping in sleeping pods designed by the architect and furniture designer Matthew Hoey—and not unlike those designed for certain first-class airlines—nappers experience relaxing music and, it is hoped, the dream state, which restores energy and restfulness *(fig. 116)*. Extremely successful in 2004, MetroNaps planned to expand to more locations in the United States and abroad.[23]

What will the bed of the future look like? Celebrity designer Laurence Llewelyn-Bowen created a virtual bed in conjunction with the Holiday Inn hotel chain. Given the task of inventing a bed that would help people not merely fall asleep but also dream, Llewelyn-Bowen produced a CAD drawing intended to create the feeling of a guest room more than a hotel room *(fig. 117)*. Carpets glow with fiber-optic lights, and the bed, looking very much like a Flou clone, is surrounded by metal organza curtains that can flutter in a breeze selected from a keypad of special effects. Lights at the sides of the bed and on the ceiling suggest sleeping under the stars. For sleeping aids, the occupant can select from among famous paintings and monumental works of architecture, which, at the push of a button, are projected onto the wall. Putting Holiday Inn at the vanguard of hotel bed design, the company has stated that such a bedroom "could be standard in 2054."[24]

Figure 114
Enzo Mari,
Tappeto volante (flying carpet).

Figure 115
Dore Gardner,
*Eighteenth Hole, Inverrary,
Florida*, 2002.

Figure 116
Matthew Hoey, MetroNaps pod,
Model 7, 2004.

Notes

1. Critical reaction to the Exhibition of Art and Industry was mixed, but most artists, art critics, and art historians were disappointed by the lack of design integrity and poor production standards. Their discontent ultimately resulted in the creation of the South Kensington Museum, now the Victoria and Albert Museum.

2. Lady Barker, *The Bedroom and Boudoir* (London: Macmillan, 1878), 33.

3. Ibid., 37.

4. Charles L. Eastlake, *Hints on Household Taste in Furniture, Upholstery, and Other Details,* 4th ed. (London: Longmans, Green, 1878; reprint, New York: Dover, 1969).

5. M. H. Baillie Scott, "A Country House," *The Studio* 19 (Feb. 1900): 37.

6. From the website www.eBay.com, August 16, 2004, text reading as follows: "Child's Simmons Wooden Maple & Iron c1890–1910 Murphy bed. This family heirloom was a transition bed for my three children from the crib. This magnificent Simmons wooden bed has Victorian-style iron hardware. It also has wooden turned legs and side supports. Additionally, it has a woven spring frame and wooden wheels. . . . It folds up easily and is easy to store."

7. Murphy's invention was successful, and he applied for a patent in 1920. Information from the website www.murphybedcompany.com.

8. Some ancient Persians actually slept on a type of water bed in which a goatskin was filled with the liquid.

9. The Canadian Broadcasting Company covered the bed-in in Montreal live during the last week of May and first week of June 1969. In a spirited exchange, newlyweds Ono and Lennon received visitors including the political activist Dick Gregory, the Quebec separatist Jacques Larue-Langlois, the singer Petula Clark, and the cartoonist Al Capp. The culmination of the bed-in was the spontaneous recording of "Give Peace a Chance," which became the anti–Vietnam War anthem. "That Was Then . . . John and Yoko's Montreal Bed-in," CBC Archives online.

10. For a thorough discussion of the relationship between these two design traditions, see *Kindred Spirits: The Eloquence of Function in American Shaker and Japanese Arts of Daily Life* (San Diego: Mingei International Museum of World Folk Art, 1995).

11. See Andrea Bocca Guarneri, *Bernard Rudofsky: A Humane Designer* (Vienna: Springer Verlag, 2003), for Rudofsky's previous writings and exhibitions concerning the bed.

12. Email communications with Edward S. Cooke, Jr., Yale University, September 2004. I thank Ned for his generous advice and fine publications on American studio furniture. See Edward S. Cooke, Jr., *New American Furniture: The Second Generation of Studio Furniture Makers* (Boston: Museum of Fine Arts, 1989), and his more recent *The Maker's Hand: American Studio Furniture 1940–1990* (Boston: Museum of Fine Arts, 2003).

13. The first Conran Shop opened in London's Knightsbridge–South Kensington neighborhood in 1964 for the "switched-on" population. Early in the twenty-first century, the Austin Powers films parodied the swinging London bedroom antics.

14. "Tots and Teens" was the name of a session I taught as part of a graduate seminar called "The Bed" that I organized for the Museum Studies division of the Fashion Institute of Technology, SUNY, New York City, in 1991. I thank those students, now colleagues, for their inspiration.

15. PR Newswire Association, press release, March 3, 1995.

16. The French ethnologist Pascal Dibie dedicated an entire chapter, "La discipline du tatami," to the French fascination with Japanese beds and bedrooms in his *Ethnologie de la chambre à coucher,* 274–285.

17. *Architectural Digest,* September 2004.

18. Information from a telephone conversation with the designers, September 11, 2004.

19. Wegner borrowed this line from a 1983 poem by Piet Hein, the full version of which is as follows: "I. Much design / is sheer disaster: / hiding what one / doesn't master. / II. True design / Asks one thing of us: / To uncover / What it covers." Hans J. Wegner, "Furniture," in *Design since 1945* (New York: Rizzoli, 1983), 120.

20. Amy Larocca, "Rock and Roll: The Delicate Art of Co-designing Lou Reed's Furniture—with Lou Reed," *New York Metro (New York Magazine)* online, April 12, 2004.

21. Information from Tamara Tjardes and Simone Ashé Morris, September 2004.

22. Dorothy Meade, *Bedrooms: Practical Bedrooms for Today* (Edinburgh: Macdonald, 1967), 63.

23. Ernest Beck, "Checking In at the Local Pod, with Plenty of Toe Room," www.nytimes.com/2004/07/22/garden/22PODS.html8hpib.

24. Front page, *City,* Rome edition, October 7, 2004.

Figure 117
Laurence Llewelyn-Bowen,
Virtual Bedroom,
CAD drawing, 2004.

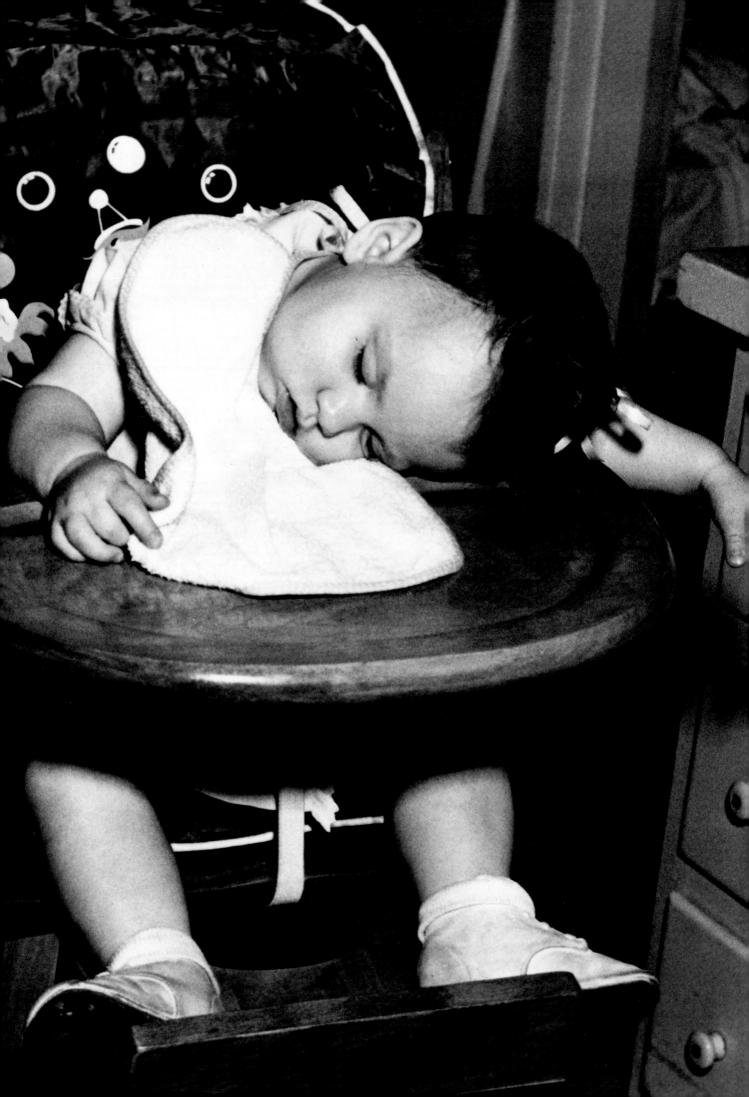

"From breakfast on through all the day / At home among my friends I stay, But every night I go abroad / Afar into the land of Nod."
—*Robert Louis Stevenson*

Bobbie Sumberg

Sleeping Small

Figure 118
William Lloyd Baab.
Susan, c. 1945.
Library of Congress, LC-USZ62-89680.

Figure 119
Baby carrier.
Borneo, c. 1950.
Rattan, wood, glass, bone,
12¼ x 13½ x 5½ in.
(31.4 x 34.6 x 14.1 cm).
Museum of International Folk Art,
gift of Diane and Sandy Besser.

Infants sleep a lot, at all times of the day and night, sometimes in seemingly anatomy-defying positions *(fig. 118)*. Gentle motion that soothes a baby to sleep has been a constant factor through time in infant sleeping arrangements. Cradle, hammock, board suspended from a tree, or pair of loving arms ensconced in a rocking chair all provide the same rhythmic movement. Portability—the ability of the mother or caregiver to take the sleeping baby along in its container—has been another feature of sleeping small through the ages.

Everywhere that people made baskets, they used them to hold infants *(fig. 119)*. The word *cradle* derives from the High German *kratto*, meaning basket.[1] Baskets woven from local materials and to the user's specifications provided inexpensive, easily portable, and disposable sleeping accommodations. The first rocking cradle may have been half a hollowed log with a naturally rounded bottom, a style that continued in use into the nineteenth century in some parts of Europe.[2]

The earliest known worked cradle with rockers came from Herculaneum, a town near Pompeii buried by successive lava flows, beginning with the famous eruption

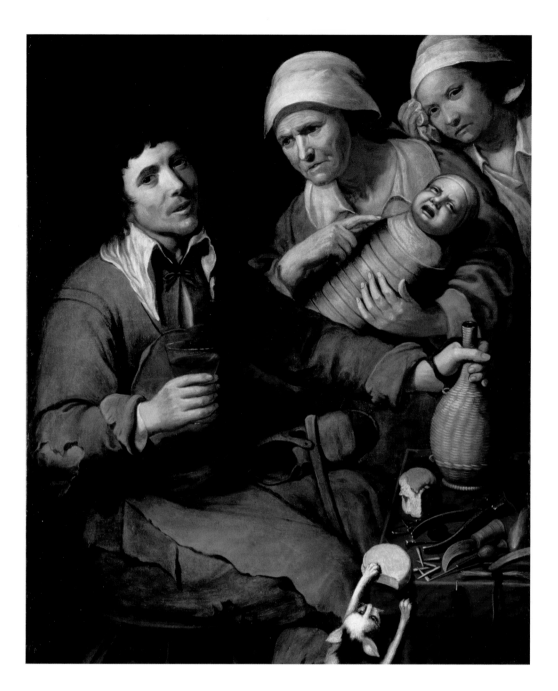

Figure 120
Master of Processions,
The Cobbler and His Family,
seventeenth century.
Oil on canvas,
41 x 33½ in. (105 x 86 cm).
Musée de la Chaussure, Romans,
France.

of Mount Vesuvius in 79 CE. Preserved in the lava were household furnishings of daily life, awaiting excavation in 1927.[3] The one rocking cradle unearthed was found in the living room of a house in the quarter called Insula Orientalis I, with a tiny skeleton inside. Leaves in the cradle indicated that the mattress was stuffed in that way. People over the centuries often used leaves and straw for cradle mattresses because the stuffing could easily be changed when soiled or incinerated to prevent contagion among other family members when a child was ill. Researchers assume that the use of rocking cradles in the Roman period was uncommon, because this is the only Roman example discovered so far.[4]

Cradles, in general use in Europe from the thirteenth century, are depicted in medieval manuscripts showing swaddled babies lying in baskets or rocking cradles. Immediately after birth, a newborn was wrapped in cloth bands with its arms straight down at its sides. Made into a compact, controlled bundle *(fig. 120)*, the infant was then tied into its cradle and rocked incessantly to keep it from complaining.[5] This practice continued until the end of the eighteenth century, and much later in some places.

Cradles up until the nineteenth century had slots or knobs on either side that were used to tie the infant bundle safely into its bed. Upper-class households employed special nurses, called rockers, who owned their cradles, to rock the babies. Family members rocked babies born into common households with one foot on the cradle rocker and hands busy with needlework or knitting.[6]

Cradles were fashioned in many styles, from absolutely plain to over-the-top ornate. Royal babies had two cradles—one for daytime lying in state and a smaller one for nighttime, both richly decorated with gold, silver, and fine textiles (fig. 121). A swinging cradle suspended from a frame that sat on the floor, from the fifteenth century, is the earliest known surviving English cradle. It is said to have belonged to Henry V.[7] Most early cradles had solid sides, and many had small hoods or roofs to keep out the greatly feared fresh air. Curtains or blankets draped over the hood further ensured the occupant's warmth. Makers often carved neatly shaped slots in either side to facilitate carrying the baby's bed from one room to another. Cradles were hung with curtains or "furniture," as bed textiles were called, in a range of fabrics: silk, velvet and "crymson cloath of Goulde" for aristocratic babies, homespun linen and wool for commoners.

The cradle crossed the Atlantic with the Pilgrims. New World cradles featured local woods such as pine, walnut, and oak (fig. 122). In colonial times, children's furniture was made by a carpenter, called a joiner (fig. 123). The end of the eighteenth century brought the demise of swaddling and a subsequent change in baby's gear. Constant rocking was no longer necessary to keep an infant pacified. Ideas about the benefits of free movement of the limbs, activity, and fresh air were popularized by the medical profession and domestic science manuals. Cradle styles with slatted or spindled sides rather than solid sides came into vogue as the general population acknowledged the health benefits of air circulation.

With this change in attitude, the practice of lulling an infant to sleep by constant rocking came under attack, and consequently the rocking cradle, too, was vilified by advocates of progressive child-rearing theories. From the insistence that mild rocking was beneficial in 1809 to the outright condemnation of rocking in 1839, the shift in attitudes toward and advice for new mothers was complete among child-rearing professionals.[8]

As the mass production of furniture grew with the development of large-scale woodworking machinery, so did the production of cradles. Growing prosperity at the turn of the nineteenth century brought cradle styles that followed furniture styles for the middle class in Europe and North America. Infants slept in empire, Gothic revival, rococo revival, Sheraton, and Eastlake cradles.

Although people still made and used cradles for newborns into the twentieth century, in the early decades of the nineteenth century the small stationary bed, called a crib, replaced the cradle for children of about a year old. Cribs had high sides with slats or spindles and were often made of painted metal. In an early development, one side could be slid down for easy removal of the child. During this period, the idea of a separate living area for children took hold among those who could afford the space. Instead of sleeping in the same room as their parents, children from infancy on were segregated in the nursery for much of the day and all of the night. This shift in the use of domestic space also produced the need for more specific children's furniture,

Figure 121
Cradle. England,
seventeenth century.
Wood, gold.
Museum of London.

Figure 122
Cradle, Virginia, USA,
late seventeenth century.
Wood.
38 x 16¼ x 23½ in.
(96.5 x 41.27 x 59.7 cm).
Museum of International Folk Art,
gift of John M. Watson.

Figure 123
Cradle. Barnstable or
Yarmouthport, Massachusetts,
1665–1685.
Red oak, white pine.
SPNEA, gift of Dorothy Armour,
Elizabeth T. Aampora, L. Hope
Carter, Guido R. Perera, Henry C.
Thacher, Louis B. Thacher, Jr. and
Thomas C. Thacher.

Figure 124
Cradle, Morzine,
Haute-Savoie, France,
c. 1800.
Wood,
34 x 19½ x 12 in.
(86.4 x 49.5 x 30.5 cm).
Museum of International Folk Art.
Gift of Direction Générale des
Relations Culturelles, France.

Figure 125
The Housewife, Japan, c.1915.
Hand-colored collotype
postcard. Private collection.

beds included. In working-class homes, however, children slept where they could, often in crowded conditions.[9]

In remote rural areas of Europe, children's furnishings, especially cradles, followed local furniture styles. Heavily carved and painted cradles with hoods and sloping sides conformed to the prevailing aesthetic and customary usage of non-industrialized agriculturalists in Europe and Scandinavia in places where factory-made and fashionable styles were unavailable or unappreciated *(fig. 124)*.

Infant and child beds can be miniatures of adult sleeping arrangements or can be specially suited to children's small sizes and varying needs *(fig. 125)*. Bedding for cradles, cribs, and children's beds differs from that used by adults mainly in size and decorative motifs but otherwise conforms to a cultural standard. In other words, an Amish crib quilt, although in miniature, follows the same stylistic pattern as an Amish quilt for a full-size bed *(fig. 126)*. Quilts were popular as bedding for both adults and children in eighteenth-century England, North America, and continental Europe. Quilts made by a mother for her children not only express her creativity and industry through choice of design and material but also embody the love and warmth with which she ideally surrounds and protects her child. The everyday sight of a child dragging a blanket along behind her affirms the idea that bedding is associated in her mind with love, warmth, and security, which are provided both by her parents and by the tangible piece of cloth, homemade or otherwise.

Figure 127
East Moravian baby cradle
(kolembač), c. 1919.
From the Ludvik Burian Collection,
accession no. 2002.73, National
Czech and Slovak Museum and
Library, Cedar Rapids, Iowa.

Figure 126
Child's quilt, Amish, USA,
c. 1890.
Cotton.
49½ x 47 in.
(125.7 x 119.4 cm).
Museum of International Folk Art,
gift of Lloyd Cotsen and
Neutrogena Corporation.

The marketing of childhood began in earnest with the Victorians and the rise of
furniture and toys mass-manufactured specifically for children. The popularity of certain
colors and design motifs thought appropriate for children was also born in the early
twentieth century. The American convention of blue for boys and pink for girls is quite
recent, codified only after World War II.[10] Clothing, nursery furnishings, and bedding
designed with age-specific decorations such as baby animals and toys and gender-
specific colorways further distinguished the cute child-size world from its sophisticated
adult counterpart. The post–World War II consumer culture also catered to an expanding
youth market. In the twenty-first century, marketing and media agencies urge families
with sufficient disposable income to spend it on decorating a child's bedroom. They
claim that doing so not only encourages a sense of style and aesthetics in a child but

also creates a significant bonding experience between parent and child through shopping.[11]

The hammock, a netted or solid textile that is suspended at each end, finds use primarily in the lowlands of Latin America and the Caribbean for sleeping and lounging. The name comes from the Arawak Indian word *hamaca*. Spanish conquistadors first encountered the word and object and brought them back to Europe, where this kind of hanging bed was unknown.[12] Sailors of the time recognized the superior comfort and space savings offered by a hammock, and it was subsequently incorporated into navy and merchant marine ships.

People living in tropical climates commonly use multipurpose hammocks as beds or chairs, and in temperate climates hammocks offer occasional summer relaxation. Zapotec Indians of the Isthmus of Tehuantepec sleep in family-size hammocks. Infants and small children share their parents' hammock while older siblings share with each other or a grandparent. Hooks are fixed to the interior walls of the house, and the hammocks are strung full length at night and hung against one wall during the day.[13] In Moravia, India, and Turkey, among many other places, hammocks serve as day beds for babies *(fig. 127)*. Although the children do not spend the night in them, hammocks are safe places for a nap or for whiling away the hours between meals—away from dangerous animals, dirt and insects on the floor or ground, and the clumsy feet of adults.

Methods of carrying an infant often do double duty as portable beds. Just as many infants in the United States are lulled to sleep while riding in a car (sometimes the only way of getting a fractious child to sleep), so the rhythm of walking and the carrier's breathing will induce a baby to sleep. Baby carriers can be as elaborate as those made by people of the Dong minority group in China, decorated with embroidery and coins *(fig. 128)*, or as simple as a braided strap that holds the child on the mother's hip, leaving her hands free for work. The Turkish hammock is also used as a method of baby transport, tied onto the mother's back. The cradle board, so called because of the wooden struts to which the cradle is tied, both holds the baby suspended from a tree or leaning against a sturdy support and allows easy carrying *(fig. 129)*. The modern-day Snugli accomplishes the same objective, that of holding the infant close to the comforting body of another human being and inducing sleep.

Sleeping arrangements—where, when, how, and with whom a baby or child sleeps—are intimately tied to cultural, social, and personal values and thus can be hotly contested. In many places in the world, infants sleep with their mothers until they are three years old or so. Whether on the floor, in a bed, or in a hammock, the mother is instantly available to tend to the child's needs and protect him or her from night terrors. In other parts of the world, people are scandalized by this idea and feel that babies should learn to sleep by themselves as soon as possible; sharing a bed with an adult is considered unhealthy and dangerous, and sharing a bed with a sibling indicates poverty. A child's ability to sleep alone is evidence of independence and maturity, and having even newborns or toddlers in their own beds gives parents a welcome break from the child's constant demands. The reemergence of the "family bed" among American parents who are exploring alternative child-raising philosophies has produced an astounding amount of controversy for such an ancient and widespread idea.[14]

Where babies sleep alone, the bassinet for a newborn and crib for an older child have replaced the cradle. Modern cribs often incorporate electronic monitoring devices, hanging toys for visual stimulation, and specially designed bedding. Youth beds, somewhat smaller than a standard twin, are still available, though not widely used *(fig. 130)*. Current trends in children's furniture lean toward full and queen-size beds, pieces that a

Figure 128
Baby carrier, Guizhou
province, China, Dong nation-
ality, c. 1930.
Cotton,
35 x 13¾ in. (88.9 x 34.9 cm).
Museum of International Folk Art,
Lois R. Livingston Bequest purchase.

child might not choose for himself but will not outgrow.[15] Bedding with motifs deemed suitable for children now makes up a large part of the market. A survey of the children's bedding choices offered by Neiman Marcus in January 2005 showed twenty-five styles, primarily florals, stripes, and geometrics, designated for girls. Of these, nineteen of the sheet, comforter, and pillow sets featured the color pink. Not surprisingly, sixteen selections for boys were predominately blue and brown, in plaids or patterned with motifs of cowboys, sports, and similar "boy" activities.[16]

Although the simplicity of a piece of cloth suspended from the ceiling contrasts with the elaborateness of a carved cradle, the effect is the same. Sleeping small is sleeping warm and protected from the physical and psychological dangers of the world as perceived by adults. These dangers vary around the globe and in parents' perceptions, producing myriad variations on the theme of sleeping small.

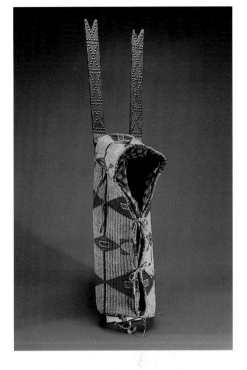

Figure 129
Cradleboard, Sioux/Cheyenne,
USA, c. 1880.
Wood, glass beads, brass nails,
sinew, parfleche, cloth, paint,
leather, umbilical cord.
46 x 10½ in. (117.2 x 27 cm).
Museum of Indian Arts and
Culture/Laboratory of Anthropology.
(9806)

Figure 130
Pinocchio bed,
New Mexico, USA, c. 1945.
Wood, paint.
68 x 36 x 42½ in.
(172.7 x 91.4 x 107.9 cm).
Museum of International Folk Art.
IFAF collection.

Notes

1. Sally Kevill-Davies, *Yesterday's Children: The Antiques and History of Childcare* (Woodbridge, UK: Antique Collectors Club, 1991), 11.

2. Lawrence Wright, *Warm and Snug: The History of the Bed* [1962] (Phoenix Mill, UK: Sutton, 2004), 169. Wright also noted some of the symbolic aspects of cradles: "The traditional wood for a cradle is birch, the tree of inception, which drives away evil spirits. A child in an elderwood cradle will pine away, or at least be pinched black and blue by the fairies. The ancient Greek child was laid in a cradle shaped like a winnowing basket, symbolizing newly harvested grain" (169).

3. See Stephan T. A. M. Mol, *Wooden Furniture in Herculaneum* (Amsterdam: J. C. Gieben, 1999).

4. Ibid.

5. Swaddling was believed to encourage good posture and an upright bearing; crawling was thought to be too animal-like. All children's furniture and accoutrements until the nineteenth century were designed to encourage early walking on the feet. See Karin Calvert, "Cradle to Crib: The Revolution in Nineteenth-Century Children's Furniture," in Mary Lynn Stevens Heininger et al., *A Century of Childhood 1820–1920* (Rochester, NY: Margaret Woodbury Strong Museum, 1984).

6. Kevill-Davies, *Yesterday's Children,* 107.

7. Ibid., 108.

8. William Buchan, MD, *Advice to Mothers on the Subject of Their Own Health: And of Promoting the Health, Strength, and Beauty of Their Offspring* (Philadelphia: Joseph Bumstead, 1809); William Alcott, *The Young Mother, or, Management of Children in Regard to Health* (Boston: G. W. Light, 1839), cited in Calvert, *A Century of Childhood,* 50–51.

9. For an interesting perspective on nurseries and children's furniture in Europe, see Ingeborg Weber-Kellermann, "A Cultural History of the Children's Room No Nursery" (sic) in *Kid Size: The Material World of Childhood* (Weil am Rhein: Vitra Design Museum, 1997).

10. In 1939, pink was advocated as a suitable color for boys, because it was a shade of red, the color associated with Mars and war. Colleen R. Callahan and Jo B. Paoletti, *Is It a Girl or a Boy? Gender Identity and Children's Clothing* (Richmond, VA: Valentine Museum, 1999), n.p.

11. Betsy Lehndorff, "A Space of Their Own: Style-Conscious Teens Put Attitude into Bedroom Makeovers," *Rocky Mountain News* online, February 12, 2005.

12. Tina Bucuvalas, "Continuity and Change in a Traditional Craft: Hammock Making among the Zapotec in Juchitan, Oaxaca, Mexico," PhD dissertation, Indiana University, Bloomington, 1986.

13. Ibid., 144.

14. The reemergence of breast feeding, and thus of a mother's need to have easy access to her baby at night, is cited as a factor in the burgeoning interest in family beds. The statistic that 95 percent of world cultures condone mothers and children sleeping together is documented in Patricia Donohue-Carey, "Solitary or Shared Sleep: What's Safe?" *Mothering: The Magazine of Natural Family Living* 114 (Sept.–Oct. 2002).

15. "Furniture 'Grows Up' in Kids' Rooms Today," *Wall Street Journal Online,* Oct. 13, 2003; "Kids' Furniture Develops a More Grown-Up Design," *Wall Street Journal Online,* Feb. 14, 2005.

16. Neiman Marcus web-based catalogue, January 27, 2005.

8. Sleeping Forever... and Ever

"Once in my room I had to stop every loophole, to close the shutters, to dig my own grave as I turned down the bed-clothes, to wrap myself in the shroud of my nightshirt." — *Marcel Proust*

Bobbie Sumberg

Sleeping Forever...and Ever

Figure 131
Caroline Gait Malim,
artist's reconstruction of a
bed burial excavated at
Barrington Anglo-Saxon
cemetery,
Cambridgeshire, c. 1998.
Pastel on paper.

Death is often likened to sleep: the grave is a bed, the mausoleum a house. Upon death, one is said to be "put to bed with a mattock, tucked up with a spade."[1] The word *cemetery* derives from the Greek *koimētērion*, meaning sleeping room.[2] Said to have originated with the story of Jesus restoring Jairus's dead daughter to life, the notion of death as sleep implies resurrection.[3]

Death has not always been associated with sleep; the idea has gone in and out of fashion over the centuries. Nevertheless, the inclusion of a bed in a tomb and the use of a bed as a coffin or as a support for a coffin have ancient origins. Five beds were discovered in King Tutankhamen's tomb, interred with his body in 1351 BCE *(see fig. 77)*. At tombs in England, excavators have uncovered burial beds used by Saxons in the late seventh century CE.[4] The bedsteads were made of ash with iron fittings *(fig. 131)*. The bed found at Edix Hill is quite narrow, about 30 inches wide, tapering at the foot to 25, and 71 inches long (76–63.5 by 180.5 cm). It is unlikely that a bed of this size was ever used for real sleeping, although a similar design in different dimensions might have

been. No actual sleeping beds remain from this period, so it is impossible to be certain how the Anglo-Saxons slept.[5]

The meaning of Saxon bed burials is unclear. Although followers of animist or "pagan" religions believed that death was the first step on a journey to another world, and therefore travelers needed household goods to help them make the journey and to furnish the afterlife, Saxon bed burials often date to the early Christian era. Whether the use of a burial bed was a holdover from pre-Christian Saxon beliefs or whether it signified something else to Christian Saxons is unknown. As the archaeologist George Speake wrote in reference to these burials, "The custom of bed-burial, whilst not exclusively aristocratic, must be seen as a variation of coffined burial, where display of the body was an important part of the burial ritual."[6]

The use of bed imagery in tomb sculpture and tomb frescos was widespread

Figure 133
Double tomb of Philipp
and Ulrich von Werdt,
St. Guillaume,
Strasbourg, France, c. 1340.

among the Etruscans, people who lived from the ninth century BCE until around 90 BCE in the area now called Tuscany in Italy. The Etruscans depicted themselves in death reposing on beds, often in banquet scenes. As in life, these beds, called *klinai*, served not only for sleeping but also for eating and relaxing. Thus the reclining figures were not asleep but in an attitude of "bliss consciously enjoyed."[7] A sarcophagus from around 285 BCE, on the other hand, depicts a couple lying in bed, not reclining on a couch *(fig. 132)*. With eyes open in a familiar embrace, husband and wife appear to be either conversing before drifting off to sleep or about to make love, in either case continuing their daily existence in the other world.

In Europe, the depiction of beds in death art declined after the Etruscans. Romans, Greeks, and early Christians were concerned with commemorating either the deceased's life or his salvation, and artists shifted from images related to providing for the afterlife to symbols associated with salvation or individual achievements. Tomb sculpture depicting reclining figures did not reappear regularly in Europe until the twelfth century, when fully three-dimensional grave sculpture again became popular. Royalty and notables had themselves depicted horizontally. From the way their clothing drapes and the position of their feet, it is clear that these figures are not in a restful pose but are standing up, though placed horizontally *(fig. 133)*. The increasing use of a pillow under the figure's head in the early thirteenth century was a transitional element that still did not suggest lying down or sleep.

The Plantagenet tombs of Henry II (d. 1189) and Eleanor of Aquitaine (d. 1204) at Fontevrault Abbey were the first to make "recumbancy 'visually explicit'" by showing garments flowing down along the body underneath, as they would if a real person were lying down.[8] But this new idea was not used widely until the next century, and even then it did not become a consistent part of the sculptor's vocabulary. During the medieval and early Renaissance periods, the idea of death was still not that of sleep. When figures were shown actually on a bed with eyes closed, they were depicted either at the moment of death, called *in transi*, or as a decayed corpse. The bed was a device for displaying the deceased's effigy, not a suggestion that death was a form of sleep.[9]

Although in use in isolated circumstances from the seventeenth century, sleep and bed imagery in association with death took off in popularity in the nineteenth century,

Figure 134
Grave marker of William P. Groot (d. 1849) and Lydia Groot (d. 1846), c. 1846. White Plains Rural Cemetery, White Plains, New York.

particularly in the United States. In the seventeenth and eighteenth centuries in North America, people generally decorated gravestones with carved religious iconography and the name and dates of the deceased.[10] Epitaphs and inscriptions were brief but pointed and usually referred to a character trait or to a fact about the deceased—as in this inscription found in Plymouth, Massachusetts: "Here / Lyeth Buried / Ye Body of Capt / Richard More / Aged 84 Years / Died 1692 / A Mayflower / Pilgrim."[11] As the nineteenth century began and progressed, references to death as eternal rest or sleep proliferated. Lem S. Frame "fell asleep in Jesus" in 1843.[12] Susannah T. George left these final words in 1872: "My feet are wearied and my hands are tired—My soul oppressed; And with desire have I long desired / Rest—only Rest."[13] Did the pace of life increase so dramatically in the nineteenth century that death was seen not as redemption but as relief and a chance to catch up on long-lost sleep?

In the large cities of Europe and North America, mourners normally buried their dead in a sanctified cemetery on church grounds. Over time, and as populations grew

Figure 135
Grave marker, c. 1849.
White Plains Rural Cemetery,
White Plains, New York.

rapidly, these cemeteries were filled to overflowing, presenting a health hazard as well as a logistical problem. The development of secular, garden cemeteries with spacious plots meant that people had room to devote to larger gravestones, mausoleums, and commemorative sculpture. Père Lachaise opened in Paris in 1804, Mount Auburn Cemetery in Cambridge, Massachusetts, in 1831, and Kensal Green in London in 1827. These new cities of the dead not only housed the bodily remains of the deceased but also provided a parklike atmosphere in which the living could enjoy a day in the country and indulge in the sentimentality the Victorians so enjoyed.

While adults were memorialized with sculpture that might be religious or secular in its iconography, they were almost never shown asleep, in bed, or even reclining.[14] The association of bed with sex was too strong to be denied and too scandalous to expose to innocent eyes. The graves of infants and children, however, were regularly decorated with beds or effigies of sleeping children. A developing ideology of the purity of children and the sanctity of the home where they resided made images of sleep and bedroom perfectly acceptable for commemorative art in the Victorian period *(fig. 134)*.[15]

A brother and sister asleep in each other's arms conveys only innocence and peace; they are angelic children who have escaped unblemished the world of commerce and depravity that awaited them in adulthood. A small empty bed *(fig. 135)* not only evokes the heartache of the parents who remain but also symbolizes, by the broken flower, the unfulfilled potential of the child's life cut short.[16] A mattress with bedding, as if on the floor, along with the inscription "Gone in the Morning," poignantly memorializes two children, "Little Steve" and "Our Josie," of Lowell, Massachusetts, the circumstances of their deaths unknown.

An extremely high mortality rate in Europe and North America during the nineteenth century contributed to a sense that death was all around.[17] The urn and the weeping willow frequently seen on tombstones from this period are often found on embroidery samplers, too, and exemplify the domestication of death in what today seems an almost morbid preoccupation.[18] Indeed, the creation of the garden cemetery as both a place to visit deceased loved ones and a public green space, promoted as a respite from the hurly-burly of nineteenth-century urban life, mirrored the growth of the idea of home, maintained by woman, as a refuge from the polluting world of male commerce. No wonder sculptures of sleeping children and epitaphs alluding to death as eternal rest or slumber blossomed during this period.

Figure 136
Burial celebration and procession. Nembe, Nigeria, 1992.

Beyond the bed and sleep imagery of monuments and tomb sculpture, the coffin itself conveys the same ideas of class, status, and style that bedroom furnishings communicate. The plain pine box is analogous to the unadorned metal bedstead of the not-well-off. The highly polished sheen, brass fittings, and quilted satin lining of the luxury box metaphorically match the carved wood and ornate curtains and furnishings of the aristocratic bed.

Beds and funerals are closely linked in some parts of Africa. The Ga of Ghana used to bury their dead in the sleeping room of the deceased's natal home, a place the deceased had always called home. The British colonial regime outlawed this practice, and the Ga people now use formal cemeteries.[19] Today, the corpse is laid on a decorated bed during a period of mourning before burial. Family and friends attend this wake-keeping and celebrate the life and achievements of the deceased.

In Nembe, Nigeria, in the delta of the Niger River, a funeral is also an occasion for celebrating a person's life and status, as well as for mourning a family's loss. During the course of the weekend needed to hold a funeral, the embalmed corpse is put in a coffin whose sides are hinged. Late on a Friday afternoon the coffin is carried to the town square *(fig. 136)* and laid on a brass bed in a small pavilion called the *duri-sun-wari*. The sides of the coffin are unhinged and folded down flat, so the corpse is effectively lying on the bed for the wake-keeping *(fig. 137)*. Folded cloths are laid on the bed next to the body, representing the obligations of the living toward the dead, the ancestors.[20] The display of the corpse on a bed in the family home or in a public place is a common feature of coastal West African funerals.[21]

The association of death and sleep extends into the mythic realm as well. Sleeping and dreaming have always been powerful symbols for other states of consciousness and unconsciousness. Plato said, "No man achieves true and inspired divination when in his rational mind, but only when the power of his intelligence is fettered in sleep or when it is distraught by disease or by some divine inspiration."[22] Sleep is a liminal state, between life and death, where the gods are active. Sleep is, in a sense, closer to death than to life, making it a perfect metaphor for both the dangers and the beauties of other realms.

Unlike a normal living human, the vampire—the undead—spends the daytime in the dark in a box of earth, only to emerge at night to search out blood-rich victims to sustain its own existence. The legend holds that a vampire sleeps in a coffin full of the dirt of his burial. Everything is reversed: the normal rhythm of day and night, grave dirt inside the box instead of outside it, and the denial of the normal process of aging and decay. That the vampire "sleeps" in a coffin as bed proves its evil, unnatural nature, bringing full circle the equation of sleep and death *(fig. 138)*.

From antiquity to the present, most people have died in a bed, whether at home or in a hospital. At the other end of life, most people are conceived and born in a bed, whatever it may look like. We spend on average one-third of our lives in bed, sometimes for extended periods of illness, rest, and recovery. Some of our most pleasurable moments and some of our most painful take place while lying in bed: moments of profound connection with a lover or the extreme dislocation of nightmare, the bliss of a hard-earned sleep or the torment of elusive slumber, the ultimate comfort and security of a warm bed to come home to or the narrowing of the world to a room with a bed filled with physical or psychic pain. The bed is essential to life and to death.

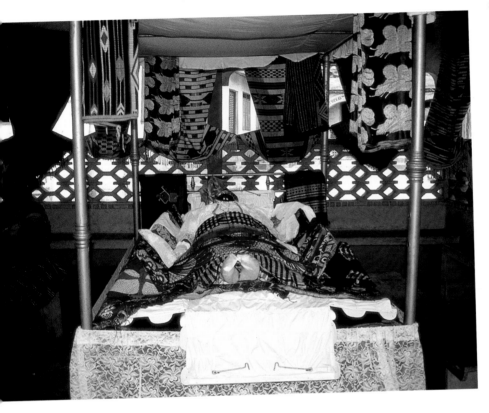

Figure 137
Wake-keeping, town square, Nembe, Nigeria, 1992.

Figure 138
Le Cauchemar de Dracula, Hammer Films, 1958.

Notes

1. Greg Palmer, *Death: The Trip of a Lifetime* (San Francisco: Harper, 1993), 7.
2. *The American Heritage Dictionary of the English Language,* 1973.
3. Noreen Marshall, "The Big Sleep," in *Kid Size: The Material World of Childhood* (Weil am Rhein: Vitra Design Museum, 1997).
4. George Speake, *A Saxon Bed Burial on Swallowcliffe Down: Excavations by F. de M. Vatcher,* English Heritage Archaeological Paper no. 10 (London: Historic Buildings and Monuments Commission for England, 1989).
5. Jacqui Watson, CfA Conservation Team, personal communication.
6. Speake, *Saxon Bed Burial,* 129.
7. Erwin Panofsky, *Tomb Sculpture: Four Lectures on Its Changing Aspects from Ancient Egypt to Bernini* (London: Phaidon, 1992), 37.
8. Quotation, ibid., 57.
9. For a full discussion of the complicated relationship between grave sculpture and societal attitudes see Panofsky, *Tomb Sculpture.*
10. For a fascinating analysis of the development of grave imagery, see Allan I. Ludwig, *Graven Images: New England Stonecarving and Its Symbols, 1650–1815* (Middletown, CT: Wesleyan University, 1966).
11. Charles L. Wallis, *Stories on Stone: A Book of American Epitaphs* (New York: Oxford University Press, 1954), 3.
12. Ibid., 58.
13. Ibid., 226.
14. There are some exceptions, of course. In Chicago's Graceland Cemetery, a mother and child are depicted on a bed. John Gary Brown, *Soul in the Stone: Cemetery Art from America's Heartland* (Lawrence: University Press of Kansas, 1994), 179.
15. Ellen Marie Snyder, "Innocents in a Worldly World: Victorian Children's Gravemarkers," in Richard E. Meyer, ed., *Cemeteries and Gravemarkers: Voices of an American Culture* (Ann Arbor: UMI Research Press, 1989), 11–30.
16. Ibid., 20.
17. In his 1860 report on life annuities and mortality, made to the comptroller general of the National Debt Office in London, Alexander Finlaison reported that one-half of all children of farmers, laborers, artisans, and servants died before reaching their fifth birthday, in comparison with one in eleven children of the landowning gentry. Cited in Sally Mitchell, *Victorian Britain Encyclopedia* (New York: Garland, 1988), 142.
18. The use of an urn to hold the ashes of the cremated body was common in ancient Greece. Since then the urn has symbolized the deceased, and the willow tree, the grief of the mourner left behind. In the United States the use of the urn and willow as funereal iconography dates to the 1760s, the Greek revival period. James Deetz and Edwin S. Dethlefsen, "Death's Head, Cherub, Urn, and Willow," *Natural History* 76, no. 3 (1967): 29–37.
19. Christine Mullen Kreamer, *A Life Well Lived: Fantasy Coffins of Kane Quaye* (University of Missouri–Kansas City Gallery of Art, 1994). Fantasy coffins are made in the shape of anything the client wants, from a fishing boat or a car to a cocoa pod. I have not, however, found a bed used as a fantasy coffin.
20. Barbara Sumberg, "Dress and Ethnic Differentiation in the Niger Delta," MA thesis, University of Minnesota, 1993.
21. See also Joanne B. Eicher and Tonye Erekosima, "Kalabari Funeral: Celebration and Display," *African Arts* 21, no. 1 (1987): 38–45, 87.
22. Quoted in Maria Ruvoldt, *The Italian Renaissance Imagery of Inspiration: Metaphors of Sex, Sleep, and Dreams* (Cambridge: Cambridge University Press, 2004), 13.

"You've made your bed, now lie in it." — *French proverb*

Photography Credits

Fig. 1 courtesy of Robert Stivers
Figs. 2, 42 courtesy of Francesca Galloway
Fig. 3 © The J. Paul Getty Museum
Fig. 4 © Robert Rauschenberg/licensed by VAGA; courtesy of Art Resource, New York
Fig. 5 photograph by Erich Lessing; courtesy of Art Resource, New York
Fig. 6, 87, 104 courtesy of Magnum Photos
Figs. 7, 125 courtesy of Shibui, Inc.
Figs. 8, 10, 12, 13, 14, 15, 18, 57, 122, 126, 129, 130 photograph by Blair Clark
Figs. 9, 17, 55, 56, 58 photograph by Pat Pollard
Figs. 11, 53, 73, 119, 128 photograph by Paul Smutko
Fig. 16 © Hiroshi Mochizuki
Fig. 19 courtesy of Throckmorton Fine Art, Inc., New York
Fig. 20 courtesy of www.spacify.com, "resource for affordable modern and contemporary furniture."
Fig. 21 photograph by Jamison Miller
Figs. 22, 24, 132 © 2006 Museum of Fine Arts, Boston
Fig. 25 courtesy of Rheinisches Bildarchiv, Cologne
Figs. 26, 33, 34, 36, 37 courtesy of Scala/Art Resource, New York
Figs, 27, 29, 35, 39, 45, 54 courtesy of V&A Images, Victoria and Albert Museum, London
Fig. 28 courtesy of Bibliothèque Nationale de France, Paris
Fig. 30 photograph by Bulloz, courtesy of RMN/Art Resource, New York
Fig. 31 © 1989 The Metropolitan Museum of Art
Figs. 32, 133 courtesy of Foto Marburg/Art Resource, New York
Fig. 38 courtesy of the Trustees of Sir John Soane's Museum, London
Figs. 41, 43 courtesy of Cora Ginsburg LLC
Fig. 46 Robert C. Lautman/Thomas Jefferson Foundation, Inc.
Fig. 48 courtesy of Christie's Images Ltd.
Fig. 49 photograph by Margot Geist
Fig. 50, 124 photograph by Addison Doty
Fig. 51 photograph by Paola Cesari
Fig. 52 photograph by J. L. Mabit
Figs. 59, 60 courtesy of Skansen
Figs 61, 62 © 1992 Nationalmuseum och Forlags AB Wiken
Fig. 63 courtesy of Nederlands Openluchtmuseum, Arnhem
Fig. 64 courtesy of Rijksmuseum, Amsterdam
Fig. 66 photograph by P. Sicard; courtesy of the Departmental Museum of Brittany
Figs. 67, 106 photograph by Antoine Lorgnier
Figs. 68 © Estate of Pavel Kuznetsov/RAO, Moscow/VAGA, New York, courtesy of Art Resource, New York
Figs. 69, 70, 71, 72, 136, 137 photograph by Bobbie Sumberg
Fig. 76 photograph by Jack Sumberg
Fig. 77 photograph by Egyptian Expedition, Metropolitan Museum of Art
Fig. 78 photograph by Joseph John Kirkbride; courtesy of the Library of Congress
Fig. 79 courtesy of bpk Berlin
Fig. 80 photograph by Francis Benjamin Johnston; courtesy of the Library of Congress

Fig. 82 photograph by Jack Delano; courtesy of the Library of Congress
Fig. 86 © Green Tortoise Adventure Travel
Fig. 88 photograph by Jeremy Cockayne
Fig. 91 photograph by Kenneth Burkhart, Chicago
Fig. 92 courtesy of Ronald Feldman Fine Arts, New York
Fig. 93 photograph by Ben Barnhart; courtesy of Ronald Feldman Fine Arts, New York
Fig. 94 used with permission of Inter IKEA Systems B. V.
Fig. 95 courtesy of Odds N Ends Waterbeds, www.AmericasBestSleep.com
Fig. 96 © Yoko Ono; courtesy of Yoko Ono/Lenono Archive
Figs. 97, 98 © Baron Wolman
Fig. 100 courtesy of Design Museum, Finland
Fig. 101 courtesy of Davis Art Slides
Fig. 102 photograph by Cary Okazaki, © Wendy Maruyama
Fig. 103 photograph by Victoria Pearson
Fig. 105 photograph by DMI/Time Life Pictures/Getty Images
Figs. 107, 108 photograph by Tony Cenicola/The New York Times
Fig. 109 photograph by M. Legall; courtesy of Kreo Gallery, France
Figs. 110, 111 photograph by Firat Erez for Derin, © Derin Company
Fig. 113 courtesy of the Paramount Hotel
Fig. 114 courtesy of Flou
Fig. 115 © Dore Gardner
Fig. 116 photograph by Nathan Sayers for MetroNaps, © MetroNaps
Fig. 117 courtesy of Intercontinental Hotel Group
Fig. 118 courtesy of the Library of Congress
Fig. 120 photograph by Michele Bellot, courtesy of RMN/Art Resource, New York
Fig. 121 © Museum of London
Fig. 123 photograph by David Carmack, courtesy of Historic New England/SPNEA
Fig. 127 © National Czech and Slovak Museum and Library
Fig. 131 © Cambridgeshire County Council Archaeological Field Unit
Figs. 134, 135 photograph by Ellen Marie Snyder Grunier

"You've buttered your bread, now sleep on it." — *Mickey Mouse*

Index

Page numbers referring to illustrations appear in italics.